Contents

In loving memory of Mr. Hoppity, my first and most intelligent little chap; Tripod, my very special three-legged friend (that no one else wanted); Flopsy, a beautiful beast of a bunny; HerMan, whose sex I was uncertain of and finally Warren(etta) who, by appearing with me on GMTV to promote The Rabbit Welfare Association's 2003 Easter campaign, 'Rabbits need SECS' (Space, Exercise, Companionship, Stimuli) inspired John Blake Publishing to contact me. I blame and thank her for getting me into this!

This book is also dedicated to my husband, Chris, and children, Dexter, Fia, Sammy and Toby who have endured months of my 'rabbitting' on.

Acknowledgements

Thanks to Anne Mitchell for all her friendly support and advice, Claire and her team at Cobham Veterinary Clinic and everyone who came to my rescue when I lost everything I had written when my computer crashed!

Thanks also to my saviours, the long-suffering Adam and Michelle and my naughty friends who forgave me for abandoning them and to all bunnies and their owners everywhere – past, present and future!

Introduction

So you want to keep a rabbit? Maybe you already have one, and want to have a better idea about how to keep it and care for it well, so that your pet has a more fulfilling life. Whatever your objective, my hope is that you will find everything you need to know about owning and caring for rabbits in the pages of this book.

I don't have an 'ology' in the subject of rabbits. I'm not a vet, a scientist or an expert of any kind. But from owning them and loving them I have a lifetime of practical experience and have gained a respectable degree of knowledge. I remember my first rabbit – Mr Hoppity – with such fondness. As a young girl, I was able to build up a bond and a sense of trust with him: I took him for walks using a harness; I let him run free in the house and garden (despite objection – he often jumped on the table during meals!); and he came whenever I called. He was, in effect, as tame and trainable as the family dog and cat, and for me it was the start of a lifelong love affair with domestic rabbits.

I have used that personal experience in writing this book, but I have also bombarded with questions every pet-shop owner, rescuer, breeder, veterinary surgeon and any other experts, and also read every book and leaflet I could lay my hands on. In writing this book I have committed myself to being thorough, and whenever opinions have differed, I have tried to find out why. I hope the result will give you a better insight into why rabbits do what they do, and how to understand their needs and their personalities. I want you to be able to spot warning signs so that you can deal with any health issues before they become serious. Most of all, I hope this will encourage you to integrate your rabbit into your family so that it becomes every bit as much a personal pet as a cat or a dog might.

WHY RABBITS?

It's official! Rabbits are the nation's third most popular pet after cats and dogs. In fact, they are rapidly becoming the 'it' pet (or should I say the rabbit pet!) of the twenty-first century. What has caused this change in trend on the pet scene and why, in recent years, have rabbits leaped so favourably into our hearts as well as our homes?

Much has to do with our change in lifestyle. Gone are the days when young mothers gave up their careers to stay at home with their 2.4 children. Times have changed: fewer women are having children, and those planning to have a family are starting later and then going back to work. Leaving a dog alone at home all day would be – well, a dog's life. They need to be walked regularly, both for the purpose of exercise and emptying. Even the best-trained will have accidents if left for too long and, if they are bored or neglected, they will resort to chewing or barking. Then there is the question of space. Modern houses have smaller, low-maintenance gardens. For practical as well as financial reasons, people are buying smaller cars. The direct impact on dogs is clear.

No wonder, then, that cats have become so popular. They are less demanding, more independent and do not need to be exercised. If they have access to a garden, they can come and go as they please through a cat flap. Cats only eat when they are hungry, so, provided there is enough food and water, they can be left at home for a few days without compromising their well-being. They are fastidiously clean and, if confined to living indoors, will happily use a litter tray. However, litter trays need cleaning out every day – sometimes more than once – which many people find unpleasant, and if there are small children about it is not particularly hygienic.

Overall, rabbits are much easier to look after, cheaper to maintain and more hygienic than dogs. Like cats, rabbits are also fastidiously clean; unlike both cats and dogs they are vegetarian, so their droppings are inoffensive and easy to clean up. Should a child mistake one for a Smartie – which is easily done! – it will do them no harm at all. As they are vegetarian, they are ideal pets for people who do not wish to keep meat in their house. With sufficient space and stimuli, rabbits can be left alone all day – although, as they are naturally sociable creatures, it would be kinder and fairer to them if they had another rabbit, pet or person for company. Admittedly they are not so easily trained or as responsive as cats and dogs, but that does not mean they cannot be wonderful pets and fabulous companions. They are bright, affectionate, inquisitive, gentle and playful – and they positively thrive in the company of people.

A BRIEF HISTORY OF RABBITS

Rabbits originated in Mongolia around 55–60 million years ago. From there they gradually spread across Asia on a migratory route that exposed them to semi-desert and desert conditions, high and low altitudes, snowy and rocky mountain ranges, lowland plains and swamplands, tropical forests and pastures. To have survived these extreme climatic and topographical – and indeed dietary – changes is a testament to their extraordinary agility and ability to adapt. Their migration was a slow process: they didn't reach Europe until around 3.5 million years ago – a seemingly small step for mankind, a giant leap for bunnykind! Fossilised footprints suggests that they were initially concentrated around the Mediterranean coasts of Spain and Portugal. They also prove that our modern pet rabbits are direct descendants of the European kind.

When and how the European rabbit arrived in Britain is subject to theory. It could be that they were originally shipped in for hunting purposes, and those that escaped bred, thereby introducing the first generation of European rabbits to our countryside. Some believe they came to Britain via France between seven and six thousand years BC when we were linked to the Continent. Others believe the Normans introduced them to our shores at the time of the Norman Conquest in 1066, although the first written references to rabbits in Britain are dated 1176.

A more popular belief is that they were introduced to Britain by the Romans, who kept and bred them in *leporaria* (enclosed pens) for meat, fur and hunting. The first people to raise and breed them domestically were French monks of the Middle Ages. Although these monks certainly kept them as a source of food, they also began the process of selective breeding as a way of developing different fur patterns and colourings. It was not until Victorian times, however, that rabbits were kept as pets.

Rabbits were first classed as *rodentia*, because of their superficial similarities to rats, mice, guinea pigs, squirrels and other rodents, but were reclassified in 1912 under the order Lagomorpha, which includes hares and pikas. The perception and understanding of rabbits changed once again about thirty years ago when it started to be understood that they can make excellent house pets, rather than needing to be cooped up in hutches.

About This Book

This book is divided up into eight sections, each one covering a separate topic essential to a complete understanding of our rabbits and their needs. I have started by offering advice about buying a rabbit: where you can buy from, what to look out for and the different breeds there are to choose from. Next, I have addressed the needs of a rabbit in terms of accommodation, feeding, grooming and healthcare. The whole purpose of having a rabbit as a pet is that it should effectively become part of the family; I have therefore examined certain behavioural problems that exist and arise, and have offered advice on how to deal with them. It is important that we understand our rabbit's physical make-up, as well as certain characteristic attributes, so this will form the basis of the next chapter. It is also essential that owners are able to recognise when their rabbit is ill, so I have included some common rabbit illnesses, their symptoms and cures. It may be that you want to start breeding rabbits, so I've made suggestions about how best to go about this and what one should be aware of.

Finally I have explored the various issues involved in having a house rabbit and how to make it safe for both you and your pet.

Owning a rabbit is immensely rewarding. I hope that this book will make it even more so.

Alice Beer

A Birthday Bunny

Having trained as a journalist, producer and director, Alice then moved into the presenter's seat and is now well established as the presenter and celebrity interviewer for the BBC's *Heaven and Earth Show* which she co-hosts with Ross Kelly, and now that she has become the proud mother of twin girls, Alice makes no secret of the fact that

she will move heaven and earth to spend as much time with them as possible.

When I was six, I knew I was getting a very special present for my birthday but I didn't know what it would be. I was thinking in terms of a pony, but, when I heard my father sawing and banging in the garden, I started to lose interest in the whole thing. No way did I want a Wendy house!

On the big day, I rushed downstairs and greedily ripped open parcels in the manner of a very badly brought-up young lady before catching sight of a huge pink bow in the garden. It was wrapped around a magnificent hutch with a large label swinging from it saying, 'HAPPY BIRTHDAY, ALICE. PLEASE WILL YOU LOOK AFTER ME?' Inside I found a beautiful grey rabbit with the longest ears and the twitchiest nose I had ever seen. I adored her.

I christened my rabbit Betty in honour of a doll from one of my reading books and she became my real-life baby. Large ears, big hind paws and a floppy tail were no barrier to dressing Betty in a fine, ready-to-wear collection of dolls' clothes, and each afternoon she was paraded around the neighbourhood in my doll's pram, tucked cosily under a white lace blanket. It was a miracle that Betty didn't just hop away at the first opportunity at such demeaning treatment, but she always stuck by me.

As the years went by, the novelty of cleaning out the

hutch wore off, but I never tired of Betty's company. She proved to be a very versatile rabbit. Having progressed from surrogate child when I was just a baby of six, she became a champion showjumper as I reached the mature age of seven. Long days were spent with my sister erecting fences and obstacle courses in the garden, and many an argument ensued over whether Betty had cheated by pushing one of the guinea pigs out of the way on the home straight.

Betty was a loving and loved pet. I never wished for any other (apart from my constant demands for that pony, which my parents had to put up with until I left school). But, when I was about nine, my father came to my bedroom one morning to break the news that Betty had run away. This started off as an inconvenience (she had always found next door's grass much greener) but as the hours wore on and we searched the streets and gardens around us, ringing on doorbells for sightings of my big, beautiful grey bunny, I gradually realised Betty wasn't coming home. I was devastated and clearly remember sobbing on my bed for hours. She was never replaced. I think I always hoped she might just pop back one day.

Later, when I was 20, I came home from university one weekend and my parents had visitors. Over lunch we were discussing a city fox that someone had spotted the night before. My father chipped in, 'Do you remember the mess that fox made when he got Alice's rabbit?'

When my baby twin girls are older, I shall get them a

rabbit, or maybe two so they can have one each – and I shall build a high electric fence around them!

Buying a Rabbit

Before you think about buying a rabbit, don't forget: the decision to buy any pet should never be taken lightly, nor should it be made by just one person if there are other people to consider. So, if it is to be a family pet, everyone should have a say in the matter.

Too often, people make the mistake of thinking that a pet bought for a child is the child's sole responsibility. Generally speaking, little children are too young to take on the chores of cleaning or feeding, and will be more interested in the pleasures their pet brings. Older children sometimes become bored once the novelty and cuteness of their pet wears off, and teenagers are prone to switching their time and affection to hobbies and friends. Parents often forget that it is therefore their job to ensure that their children are looking after their pets properly, and that they themselves could end up with the responsibility.

What type of pet you choose depends on a number of factors: your lifestyle, the accommodation you can offer, the amount of outdoor space you have, and, of course, that oft-forgotten issue of compatibility with existing pets. When all these factors are taken into account, rabbits often emerge as a popular choice; nevertheless, you must always be sure that you will have the time, energy and enthusiasm to devote to whichever pet you choose.

Once you have decided that a rabbit really is for you, you will need to decide which breed(s) will be suitable for you.

BREEDS

The decision to buy a pure-bred or a mixed-breed rabbit is entirely personal, and there are positives and negatives in either. Pure-bred rabbits are not necessarily 'better' than mixed breeds, but there are a few reasons why you might want to choose a pure breed to start with:

APPEARANCE

With a pure-bred rabbit, you will have a very good idea of how it will look, how big it will grow and how much attention its coat will need.

BREEDING

If you intend to breed rabbits as a hobby, it is best to start off with pure breeds – the aim of a responsible breeder should be to improve the breed, not to mix it indiscriminately.

CHARACTER

Some breeds are naturally docile, while others are more playful and some show signs of being aggressive. By selecting a particular pure breed, you will have a basic idea of the character it will develop.

EXHIBITING

Certain pure breeds are particularly prized for exhibitions, so if this is your aim, do your research – the more popular the breed, the greater the competition, so you need to think carefully about the breed you select.

On the other hand, there are advantages to having a mixed-breed rabbit. If you decide to go for a rescue animal, or get one from a pet shop,you are much more likely to take home a mixed-breed rabbit, as they are more prevalent in both these places. The other consideration is that pure-bred rabbits are all almost identical within their breed, whereas mixed-breeds are all unique. So if you want a special rabbit, then a mixed breed is for you!

There are a large number of breeds recognised in the UK. The following is a rough guide to the majority of them:

ALASKA

Distinguished by their black, silky fur, matt-black bellies and dark-brown eyes, Alaska rabbits weigh between 3 and 4 kilograms. The breed is a cross between Argente and Himalayan, and the rabbits' pretty looks make them popular pets, although they are not necessarily the easiest to handle.

ANGORA

These beautiful rabbits, believed to have originated from Turkey around a hundred years ago, are one of the oldest known breeds of domestic rabbit. Angora rabbits are instantly recognisable by their long, luxurious fur, prized for being the lightest and softest wool produced by any animal, and it is for this that they are often bred.

Angora rabbits make gentle pets, but they are high maintenance. Their long, fine fur mats and knots easily, so they need to be brushed and combed each day, and require regular clipping and cleaning, especially when they are moulting.

There are five varieties of Angora rabbit, which come in twelve different colours (apart from the Giant Angora), and all of them are gentle and soft-natured:

English Angora
This is the smallest of the Angoras, weighing an average of 2.75 kilograms. The fur is incredibly fine, but this variety does not produce as much wool as the others. The English Angora is as gentle as it is soft, and is therefore much desired as a pet.

French Angora
This was the first Angora to be bred specifically for its wool. French Angoras are slightly larger than English Angoras, weighing an average of 3.6 kilograms, but they are less fluffy and consequently do not need quite so much maintenance.

German Angora
German Angoras are slightly larger than French Angoras, weighing approximately 4 kilograms.

Satin Angora
A popular choice as they are by far the easiest to groom.

Giant Angora

Like the English Angora, the fur of the Giant Angora is long and lovely; they are always white and have either blue or red eyes.

ARGENTES

There are four varieties of Argentes, all of which originated in France. Latterly they have been bred for meat, but they were originally bred for their fur.

Argente Bleu

The off-white top coat, with lilac undertones, gives the Argente Bleu a bluish hue, hence its name. It weighs around 2.75 kilograms.

Argente Brun

Like the Argente Bleu, the Argente Brun weighs around 2.75 kilograms, but it became extinct soon after it was exported from France in the 1920s. The breed was recreated around 1939, but it is still extremely rare.

Argente Champagne

This is the oldest fur breed in the world, and the largest of the Argentes, weighing around 3.5 kilograms. It was introduced into England in 1919, but had been common in the Champagne region of France for 300 years before that. It is the province, therefore, rather than their colour that gives them their name as they are in fact black.

Argente Crème

This is the smallest of the Argentes, weighing 2.25 kilograms, and so named because of the creamy colour and pale orange undertones of its fur.

BELGIAN HARE

The Belgian Hare originates from Flanders in northern Belgium and looks like a hare but, despite its name and looks, is in fact a rabbit. It is one of the earliest fancy breeds, although it has also been bred for its meat, and is reputed to be the most intelligent of all rabbits. Its lean body, long legs and ears, elegant posture and short, chestnut-coloured coat makes the Belgian a prized fancy breed. It was first brought to England in 1874, and weighs between 2.75 and 4.6 kilograms.

BEVEREN

This is one of the oldest and largest fur breeds in existence, and is found in five colours: blue, black, white, brown and lilac. First bred in the early 1900s, these rabbits originate from Beveren, a small town outside Antwerp in Belgium. Their size and their thick, silky, shiny coat turned them into a major source of fur, but they also provided meat and became particularly popular in the UK during the First World War when meat was scarce. Now Beverens are sought-after pets: their good nature makes them particularly suitable for children.

BLANC DE BONSCAT

An enormous rabbit: the buck weighs a minimum of 5 kilograms; the doe a minimum of 5.5 kilograms. It was introduced to England by commercial rabbit farmers, but it is less common as a pet.

BLANC DE HOTOT

The Blanc de Hotot originated in France, around 1902, where it is still very popular, although it didn't become popular in the UK until around 1960. It weighs between 4 and 4.5 kilograms.

BRITISH GIANT

The British Giant is the largest breed recognised in the UK. These rabbits weigh upwards of 5.7 kilograms, and their colouring ranges from black to dark grey, brown-grey, pale-grey to white. They make great pets, but obviously need lots of space.

CHINCHILLA

The Chinchilla rabbit closely resembles the real chinchilla – a small South American rodent with similar fur and colouring. Chinchilla rabbits originated in France in 1913 and first came to the UK after the First World War. Their fur is extremely soft and silky, and consists of three shaded tiers: the base is a bluish tone, the middle is a pearl-grey and the top is white, tipped with black guard hairs. They weigh between 2.5 and 3 kilograms.

CHINCHILLA GIGANTA

As the name suggests, these look very much like the standard Chinchilla, only bigger. But the fur is not quite as shiny, and the top coat is slightly darker.

DEILENAAR

The Deilenaar rabbit, bred by the Dutch in the late 1930s, is a cross between a Belgian Hare, a Chinchilla and a New Zealand. It weighs between 2.5 and 3 kilograms.

DUTCH

Dutch rabbits weigh up to 2.5 kilograms and are bred in eight colours: black, blue (the most popular), chocolate, yellow, tortoiseshell, pale grey, brown-grey and steel-grey. They all have white paws and a distinctive white band that runs from the front of the nose to form a broad collar around the neck. They are judged by their markings, but if they are sub-standard, they are often sold off as pets. They are reputed to be fantastic foster mothers.

ENGLISH

This medium-sized breed is one of the oldest fancy breeds and has been popular for over 100 years. The does have exceptionally strong maternal instincts, and so make wonderful foster mothers and incredibly affectionate pets. I know because I have one and Patchy Petra (P.P. for short) is all of these things and more. She looks after Sherman my guinea pig as if he were her own child, washing behind his ears each day and finding him when they run around the house together. She is equally affectionate with us, and nothing would please her more than to be able to show affection to our cats and dog. Sadly they are less forthcoming.

English rabbits weigh around 3.6 kilograms and are traditionally white with coloured spots around the body in either black, blue, tortoiseshell, grey or champagne, with their ears, backbone and distinctive butterfly pattern on the nose in the same colour.

FLEMISH GIANT

The Flemish Giant originated in Flanders, where it was known as the Patagonian, and is the second largest breed in the world after the English Giant. The standard dark-steel-grey coat – the only colour officially recognised in Britain – is uniformly thick and bright. Bucks weigh a minimum of 5 kilograms; does a minimum of 5.4 kilograms. In other countries they are bigger and bred in different colours.

FOX
There are five varieties of Fox rabbit – silver, black, blue, chocolate and lilac – and their weight ranges between 2.5 and 3.25 kilograms. The Silver Fox is one of the most popular fur breeds and was the first to be exhibited in 1926. The other colours were also exhibited shortly afterwards.

GIANT PAPILLON
The French version of the British Giant, the Giant Papillon weighs between 5.5 and 6 kilograms, which makes it slightly smaller but nonetheless gigantic compared with other large breeds.

HARLEQUIN
Originally known as the Japanese, the Harlequin was bred from a Tortoiseshell Dutch for exhibiting in France. For a short while the fur became a stylish fashion statement and the meat a filling meal during the Second World War. Now it is one of the more popular patterned breeds. There are eight different two-tone chequered varieties, all weighing up to 3.6 kilograms.

GLAVCOT
The Golden Glavcot is a derivative of the original Silver Glavcot.

Both became extinct around the 1930s, but the Golden Glavcot was recreated after an absence of forty years. It weighs around 2.5 kilograms.

HAVANA

The ancestry of the Havana is unknown – the only reason it shares a name with the Cuban capital is because the brown colouring of the fur is the same colour as the country's cigars. In the dark, their big brown eyes glow ruby red.

HIMALAYAN

The Himalayan is one of the oldest fancy breeds; it is also widely used in laboratory tests. Himalayans have long bodies, red eyes and short white fur with black, chocolate-brown or blue markings on their ears, feet, nose and tail. They weigh from 900 grams to 2.1 kilograms, and their docile nature makes them extremely good pets.

ISABELLA

The Isabella rabbit was bred in the UK in the late 1920s for its fur, but after the decline of the fur trade it fell from favour in England. It was exported to Holland in 1940 as the Beige, then reimported to England in the 1980s as the Isabella.

LILAC

Bred in Cambridge in 1910 and first exhibited in 1913, the Lilac rabbit was originally called the Cambridge Blue. It is a pretty dove-grey colour and weighs up to 3 kilograms. Although the fur is dense and silky, it wasn't a hit with furriers; nor, strangely enough, has it been very popular as a pet, despite being one of the more docile breeds.

LOP

Lops are the oldest breed in the world to be exhibited, and are also generally recognised as the oldest breed of domesticated rabbits. The hallmark of all lops is their long, droopy ears – some are so long they drag along the ground! Lops are usually short-haired but, as a result of breeding with other types of rabbit, several varieties have longer hair. All are gorgeous, and their gentle nature makes them hugely popular pets. There are a number of varieties:

English Lop

The English Lop was the first of all Lops and remains the most popular. It is slightly smaller than the French Lop, but has the largest ears of all rabbits.

French Lop

The French Lop is the largest variety of Lop, weighing up to 6.8 kilograms. It is a cross between the English Lop (but has shorter ears) and the Flemish Giant.

Dwarf Lop

A cross between the French Lop and the Netherland Dwarf, the Dwarf Lop originates from the Netherlands and is the second most popular exhibition breed after the Netherland Dwarf. It weighs between 2 and 2.5 kilograms.

Cashmere Lop

This is a long-haired version of the Dwarf Lop.

Danish Lop

The Danish Lop is similar to the French Lop, but no longer exists as a breed in the UK.

German Lop

The German Lop is a smaller version of the French Lop, weighing 3.2 kilograms.

Meissner Lop

The Meissner Lop is the most recent variety of Lop. It has a distinctive silver colouring and weighs between 3 and 4 kilograms.

Mini Lop

The Mini Lop is the smallest of all lops, produced from breeding the smallest French Lop with the smallest of Dwarf Lops, and weighs between 1.4 and 2 kilograms.

NETHERLAND DWARF

Also known simply as the Dwarf, the Netherland Dwarf is considered the favourite breed of all rabbits. Unfortunately they are also more likely to suffer from malocclusion of the teeth than most, but the problem is slowly being eradicated. The tiny ears and stocky little body, which weighs no more than 1.1 kilograms, make the Dwarf easy to handle and suitable for little children and older people. The does are exceptionally docile; the bucks, on the other hand, can be surprisingly bad-tempered!

NEW ZEALAND
The New Zealand rabbit comes in four varieties:

New Zealand Red
With its reddish-tan fur, this variety was originally bred in America for its meat. The first of the New Zealand varieties, it weighs around 3.5 kilograms.

New Zealand White
This albino is larger than the New Zealand Red, weighing between 4 and 5.4 kilograms. Although fairly popular as an exhibition breed, it is more popular than any other in the world for meat, and is also regularly used for laboratory tests.

New Zealand Black
The New Zealand Black is the same as the New Zealand White in every respect other than colour.

New Zealand Blue
The New Zealand Blue is also the same as the New Zealand White in every respect other than colour.

PERLFEE
The Perlfee is a German rabbit descended from the Havana. Weighing about 2.5 kilograms, it is an attractive lilac-grey, although not very popular as a pet.

POINTED BEVEREN
The Pointed Beveren, never popular, became extinct in the

1930s, but was brought back in the late 1980s. It is a very rare breed. The marked difference between it and the original Beveren breed is that it has white-tipped hairs and claws.

POLISH

An attractive small rabbit weighing between 1.1 and 1.4 kilograms. It used to be fed on milk and meal to produce the most luxurious meat for gourmet rabbit stews, but is now bred for show. The fur is very short and looks as if it has been shined to a polish – hence the name, although it is pronounced like the adjective for Poland. The most usual and popular variety is the Red-Eyed White, but they are also bred in black, blue, smoke and sable. The Polish has a reputation for being rather lively and sometimes bad-tempered, so it is not considered suitable for children or novices.

REX

The Rex comes in a wide variety of colours and is immensely popular both for exhibiting and as a pet. Its coat is shiny and velvety, thanks to its short guard hairs and short undercoat.

RHINELANDER

The Rhinelander was first imported to England from Germany in 1965, but it remains a fairly uncommon breed. Its base colour is white, but it has black and orange markings around the base, back and sides.

SABLE

There are two varieties of Sable rabbit: the Marten Sable and the

Siamese Sable. Each comes in three shades – light, medium and dark – and both are very placid which makes them great pets.

SALLANDER

The Sallander originated in Holland in 1975 and was introduced into England in 1994, making it one of the most recent breeds brought into this country. It is a thick-set, well-rounded bunny weighing between 2.5 and 4.25 kilograms. Apart from the pearl-coloured fur and darker grey guard hairs, it is identical to the Thuringer.

SATIN BREEDS

Satin Breeds were developed in the United States and derive from the Havana. They were imported into England in 1947 and come in ten different colours: black, blue, Californian, chinchilla, chocolate, copper, red, Siamese, white and broken (ie, white broken with coloured fur patterns). They weigh between 2.7 and 3.6 kilograms, and have been crossed with the Rex to produce the Satin Rexes.

SIBERIAN

Produced as a fur breed in the 1930s, the Siberian is no longer popular with furriers, although it is a sought-after fancier's choice and is produced in black, blue, brown and lilac.

SILVER

The Silver is one of the earliest exhibition breeds and is now one of the most popular with hobbyists. It originated in France, where it was known as the Riche, meaning rich or valuable. These beautiful rabbits have short, evenly spread glossy fur. They are produced in four colours but are made all the more distinctive by the subtle silvery highlights that start to appear after the first moult, several months after they are born. They weigh from 1.8 to 3 kilograms and are hardy. They are also considered an ideal pet for older children, who find the silvering process fascinating. There are a number of varieties:

Silver Grey

The first example of this breed, the Silver Grey mysteriously disappeared and then reappeared in 1860, living wild in warrens around Lincoln.

Silver Fawn

This was produced some time later in the UK by crossing a Silver Grey with a Fawn.

Silver Brown

This is a cross between a Silver Grey and a Belgian Hare.

Silver Blue

The Silver Blue was the last variety to be produced, around 1980.

SQUIRREL

This pretty animal, which resembles the Siberian squirrel, is a cross between a Chinchilla and an Argente Bleu. It was bred for beauty and the fur trade loved it. However, breeding stopped soon after it was created in the 1920s, but it was recreated in the 1980s. It weighs around 3.4 kilograms.

SUSSEX

A relative newcomer, the Sussex was produced, as its name suggests, in rural Sussex, England, as a fur breed in 1986. It weighs around 3.4 kilograms. The Sussex Gold was standardised in 1991 and the Sussex Cream was introduced later.

SWISS FOX

Of Swiss/German origin, this rare breed is kept going by the Swiss, who introduced it to Britain in the early 1980s. It has a short neck and weighs between 2.5 and 3 kilograms. The most common colours are white, black, blue and dark brown, but, because of its dense coat and long hair, it isn't a very practical breed of rabbit to own.

TAN

One of the oldest breeds, the Tan came into existence after domestic rabbits got into a warren of wild rabbits. The original ones were black – blues, chocolates and finally lilacs were developed at a later stage.

THRIANTA

The Dutch-bred Thrianta gained recognition in Holland after the Second World War and in England in the early 1980s. Despite its brilliant reddish-orange colour, it isn't a particularly popular breed.

THERINGER

A cross between a Himalayan and an Argente, the Theringer was originally bred in Germany and imported into England in the late 1960s. It weighs around 3.5kg and is a buff-yellow colour with bluish-black guard hairs mainly found around the tufty rear end.

VIENNA BLUE

The Vienna is an old Austrian breed dating back to the 1890s. It is produced in white, black, grey, blue-grey and blue, but only the Blue is recognised in the UK. The Vienna Blue weighs from 3.5 to 5.5 kilograms and is without doubt one of the most popular breeds for exhibiting and owning.

SIZE

It is common knowledge that, if you look at the size of a puppy's paws in relation to the size of its body, you will get a rough idea of how large it will grow – if the paws are proportionately larger than the puppy's body, it's likely you'll have a large dog further down the line. Unfortunately, this does not apply to baby rabbits!

Before you buy a baby rabbit, it will help to know how large it will grow. With mixed breeds, this can be difficult, although seeing the parents will be an indication, whereas with pure breeds, the size is obviously more consistent.

Rabbit sizes are divided into four classifications – small, medium, large or giant – as follows:

- Small: up to 2.5kg
- Medium: up to 4kg
- Large: up to 5kg
- Giant: upwards of 5kg

Small rabbits are more manageable, but they can be easily lost or trapped in small spaces. Medium rabbits are a perfect compromise: they are easy to handle and can be transported in small carry boxes. Large rabbits need lots of space and large accommodation. Although wonderful to cuddle up to, Giants are too heavy for small children to carry, and standard pet carriers are basically too small to transport them.

The size of a rabbit also has an effect on its life expectancy. In the wild, rabbits live an average of three to four years, although in reality certain factors such as disease, birth defects, accidents and predators often prevent them from living beyond one or two years. Domestic rabbits, on the other hand, can live between three to ten years, depending on the size and breed. As a rule of thumb, the bigger the breed or the larger the litter from which the rabbit comes, the shorter the lifespan. (Another rule of thumb is that pure breeds don't usually live as long as mixed breeds.)

For the largest breeds such as the Giant Papillion, Flemish Giant and French Lop the average lifespan is three to four years; medium breeds such as the Californian, Alaskan, Viennese and medium-sized mixed breeds live for an average of five to six years; and the smallest such as the Polish and the Netherland Dwarf can live for up to ten years. However, any rabbit kept in good health can live to well in excess of these averages.

BOYS OR GIRLS?

Personally, I've never had a particular preference as to which sex of rabbit I have – I am more influenced by how a rabbit looks and how it responds to me. Both sexes have their pros and cons and I love them equally! Given the choice, though, there are certain things to consider. There is no question that males and females do have different personalities and, although they both make wonderful pets, they both have downsides that you should be aware of. Dominant male rabbits can be aggressive, both towards people and other rabbits. They can also be distracted by their constant desire to breed! Males also have a rather unpleasant habit of marking their territory with their urine. Females, on the other hand, are more hormonal and therefore more prone to mood swings. Because they protect their young, they are more inclined to be highly territorial, yet their maternal instincts make them naturally more friendly and gentle. However, these sex-related characteristics can be counteracted by castrating the males and spaying the females.

YOUNG OR OLD?

There's no denying it: baby rabbits are infinitely more cute and cuddly. But cootchy-coos and looks aside, bringing home a baby rabbit does have certain advantages: being small, it is easy to handle; it learns to bond from an early age and to build up trust as it grows. Also, training from scratch is understood and achieved more quickly.

Adopting a previously well-cared-for adult also has its advantages: it is used to being handled and is therefore less afraid; it is used to people and is more socially adept; it is less wary of common smells and noises; and with age rabbits naturally become calm and confident. You will have also escaped the problems associated with puberty and adolescence. If the rabbit has been neutered or spayed, so much the better – you are spared the expense and the trauma and, if it has also been house-trained, that is an extra bonus!

The transition from one owner to another can be made much easier for you – and ultimately the rabbit – if you adopt the same language, same diet and basic level of care as the rabbit has grown accustomed to. However, adults that have been mistreated or less well cared for in the past quite often come with their individual problems. Building trust takes a lot of patience, sympathy and understanding.

HOW TO SPOT A HEALTHY RABBIT

It is important to make a few preliminary checks to ensure you are buying a happy and healthy rabbit. These tips will help to assess your potential rabbit's general health and sociability:

- Spend time handling the rabbit you have set your heart on. A nervous kitten or adult is likely to have been handled badly, or not at all. Consequently, it will be harder to handle at first and it will take longer before it is tame, so be aware that you need to devote more time and have the patience to build up its confidence and trust.
- Rabbits are ready to leave the nest when they reach around six to eight weeks old. Taken too young, they will be more nervous and their social skills will be underdeveloped.

Furthermore, if they are not fully weaned, they may also suffer from mild malnutrition.

- Check the rabbit's eyes, ears, feet, fur, anus, nails and teeth. Weepy eyes, crusty ears, sore hocks, dull fur, split nails or matted or stained fur around the anus clearly denote superficial or more serious underlying problems. Long teeth are almost certainly due to a dislocated jaw.
- Observe how the rabbit socialises with others in the litter and interacts with you.
- Look at the rabbit's living conditions, and state of the mother and litter mates. Unhygienic living conditions can lead to familial illnesses and diseases.

Once you have decided which breed is suitable for you, there are a number of places you can go to buy your rabbit.

BREEDERS

Breeders are primarily the best source of healthy, pure-bred rabbits. They are extremely knowledgeable and will be able to help you choose the right one for you. They will probably be able to introduce you to the rabbit's parents so that you can check it is from good, healthy stock and get some idea about how your rabbit's personality is likely to develop. More importantly, with a few exceptions, breeders are likely to have taken very good care of all their rabbits.

Before you decide on a breeder, however, it is important that you take a few precautions. Most recognised breeders are bona fide, but they are also in the business of making money out of breeding, so don't be lured into thinking they are entirely unbiased. It is a good idea to call in advance to get a feel for the breeder's operation. Ask how many rabbits the breeder currently has and whether they look after them by themselves. Caring for animals is time-consuming and, if they are caring for too many, it is likely that corners are being cut. If they seem knowledgeable and responsible, ask if you can visit their premises. If they seem reluctant, they probably have something to hide.

Here are a couple of things you should take into consideration when going to a breeder:

WHAT IS THE CONDITION OF THE MOTHER?
If the mother is there to be seen, pay good attention to her condition. Pregnant and nursing mothers need more food and water to meet the demands of their hungry little babies. If the mother looks emaciated, it is likely she has not been properly cared for and will have struggled to feed her babies, who in turn will be in poor health.

WHAT ARE THE RABBIT'S CURRENT LIVING CONDITIONS LIKE?
If the home and bedding is dirty, babies are at a greater risk of picking up illnesses and diseases, so much of your time (and money) will be spent at the vet's.

See the Appendix on page 211 for advice on how to locate breeders.

PET SHOPS

If you are after a mixed-breed rabbit, a pet shop is normally your first point of call, but don't be surprised if you also come across pure-bred rabbits in there as well – they can be a useful outlet for breeders who want to sell rabbits that don't come up to exhibiting standards. A word of warning, though: pet shops trade on the impulse buy. I'm sure there are plenty of people who have gone in for a tub of goldfish food and walked out with a rabbit.

Pet shops have one distinct advantage over other outlets: convenience – you can buy everything your rabbit needs in one place. However, all is not rosy. There are good pet shops and bad ones, and you need to be able to tell one from the other. It is in the interests of the pet-shop owner – rather than the animals – to sell their stock as quickly as possible while they are still young and appealing. As a result of this, too many are sold to potentially unsuitable owners. When it comes to sourcing stock, sometimes less care is taken than ought to be, so there are certain things to look for and questions you should always ask when you are buying from any pet shop:

WHO DID THE PET SHOP GET THE BABIES FROM?

If the pet-shop owner doesn't know where they came from, they won't know what they have taken on – and neither will you.

HOW MANY TIMES HAS THE PET SHOP TAKEN RABBITS FROM THE SAME SOURCE?

Rabbits are highly fertile, and there is often a temptation for people to make easy money through intensive breeding. If stock is regularly being taken from the same source, the chances are that the parents are being overbred, or even interbred. This weakens the strain and heightens the risk of birth defects being passed on from generation to generation.

WHAT BREED OR SIZE WERE THE RABBIT'S PARENTS?

Are they small, medium or large? It will give you an indication of what sort of size your rabbit will grow to. It is perfectly reasonable for you to want to know this sort of information, so, if the pet-shop owner can't give it to you, ask for the number of the breeder. If they are reluctant to hand this over, it begs the question why.

Three years ago my children bought me a rabbit called Warren for Christmas. The pet shop sold the rabbit to them knowing full well that he was a dehydrated, anorexic, mite-infested, weak little thing with a dislocated jaw. To add insult to injury, they said that they would replace him or refund their money if he died. On top of that, he turned out to be a she! Although it was irresponsible of the pet-shop owner to sell her, and I was confronted with huge veterinary bills, we loved Warren (or Warrenetta as we renamed her!) all the more for her defects! Against all odds, she lived for over three years – far beyond everyone's expectations.

That said, I most certainly do not want to put you off buying a rabbit from a pet shop. Most are responsible, clean and well run, and will generally tell you if a rabbit has any issues that you need to be aware of.

RESCUE CENTRES

There are about 250 rescue centres in the UK, and the managers of each and every one know all too well the sadness of taking in unwanted pets and the difficulties of rehoming them. Rescue centres are charitable organisations and the people who run them do so out of the kindness of their hearts and the love of rabbits, not for money. Sadly, rescue centres are nearly always full, mainly with abandoned, unwanted and impulse-buy bunnies. When difficulties arise, many owners assume that their pet is the cause of the problem. In fact, there are very rarely 'problem' rabbits. More usually, there are problem owners who do not fully understand the ways and needs of their rabbits.

The only disadvantage of rescue centres is that the history of the rabbit and its previous owner is not always known. However, these centres always do a thorough health check, and whatever information they do have about any rabbit in their care is passed on to the potential owner. The last thing the rescue centre wants is for the rabbit to be returned, so the likelihood is that it will be them asking you the questions, rather than the other way around. If you don't appear to be a suitable owner for a particular rabbit, don't be surprised if they refuse to let you have one, or that you come away with one that you hadn't considered. It could be that you wanted a baby so you could watch it grow up, but instead you end up with an adult rabbit. Or you might have wanted a long-haired pedigree and instead you become the owner of a short-haired mongrel! By assessing you and your situation, they will help you find the right rabbit, so keep an open mind.

You may be asked for a small donation of between £10 and £20 to help towards running costs. So, go on, give an abandoned bunny a loving home!

VETERINARY SURGERIES

Whenever I am sitting in the vet's waiting room, I am struck by the number of animals being advertised on the noticeboard, especially kittens, puppies and rabbits. The parent animals are often registered with the clinic, so you can be sure that their healthcare has been a priority, and often they are offered free of charge. It's not a bad idea to ask the seller if you can take the rabbit on approval – most vets will give them a basic health check for a small fee, which will give you peace of mind.

FRIENDS

One of the advantages of getting a baby rabbit from a friend is that you will have the opportunity to examine the mother and nest companions. Friends are also more likely to be honest about any health problems the litter may have had, as well as being open about the pros and cons of owning a rabbit. One word of warning, though: many children become keen to have a rabbit because their friends have one. There is nothing wrong with this per se, but parents should make sure they think through the implications fully before agreeing to their child's demands!

Toyah Willcox

Rabbits Rule

Since bursting on to the scene as a punk rock singer in the 1970s Toyah's career as a singer and songwriter was complemented by her becoming an actress on stage, TV and screen, starring in films such as *Quadrophenia* and *Jubilee*. In 2003 she braved the jungle in *I'm a Celebrity, Get me out of Here!* then embarked on an

exhausting tour of the West End play *Calamity Jane*. Away from the limelight, she lives quietly in Worcester with her husband, Crimson Rock star Robert Fripp, and her companion rabbit.

All I wanted for my ninth birthday was a rabbit, but my parents would not allow any pets in the house and, as I was the youngest child, they didn't want to spoil me. But when my birthday arrived we were on a family boating holiday on the River Avon, and as a treat my parents took me to a pet shop in Tewkesbury that had baby rabbits for sale. There were about nine, all cramped inside a little hutch, but there was one, a white New Zealand, that was so spirited and spunky. I immediately fell in love with him. It was an instant spiritual bond and, from that day onwards, Snowy and I were inseparable.

He played outside in the covered yard, but the rest of the time he lived in my bedroom. Every morning when I woke up I would call his name and he would come running. In time, every rabbit will come when it is called and will learn to understand 'Yes' and 'No'. Snowy was so affectionate towards me, but to anyone else he was outstandingly ferocious. One day I saw him sink his teeth into my brother Kim's stomach, but with me he was entirely different. I think he was jealous and thought of me as his wife!

I should never have let Snowy get away with his aggression, but I was too young to handle it so I never did anything to stop him. That's why, however much a child may want a rabbit, I would never recommend it and would do everything in my power to dissuade parents from letting them have one. I feel so strongly about it, I would even go so far as stealing a rabbit if I thought the child was too young or the rabbit wasn't being cared for properly! I wouldn't consider letting a child under twelve own a rabbit – they don't fully understand what pain is or know how to associate with pain. Children think rabbits are furry little toys or like cats and dogs, which they are not.

Rabbits are timid but very social little creatures. They were born native and should be kept in an environment that stimulates them. The same goes for mice and rats. I am hugely relieved that adults have also fallen in love with rabbits and are eager to own them as pets. It's the ones that are sold to children that invariably end up as unwanted pets, but the pet shops are as much to blame for that as the parents.

When we got Snowy the pet shop didn't tell us anything! Fortunately my mother had had a couple of rabbits as a child so she had a little bit of knowledge. The rest I learned myself from watching him and seeing what he wanted and needed. Despite that, I continued buying from pet shops, as they knew what I wanted and knew where to find them. But, from now on, I will go straight to the breeders so I can see the parents.

Since Snowy, I have only owned New Zealand whites and they have all been male. They're huge – the size of a small dog – but not very robust. White ones have weak hearts and weak eyes so they don't live longer than six years. It's heartbreaking, but I know what to expect so I have to accept that. Male rabbits are easier to train and I love their bombastic character. They're completely driven by their sexuality and are so comical. Females don't look so appealing with their dewlap [the floppy roll of skin under their chin] and when they're broody or nesting I don't feel very sympathetic, I'm afraid to say.

My sister Nicola became interested in rabbits after I got Snowy, but waited until she left home before she bought her first one. She always has Giants – the biggest breed there is. They are massive, like a Shetland pony, but they only live for around two years. She loves rabbits as much as I do and has the same relationship with them as I have with mine, and we have only ever kept our rabbits as house pets.

I know chewing is the biggest downside of owning a rabbit, but it doesn't bother me at all, so I don't see it that way. Mine have chewed through all the wiring, but my last rabbit, Beaton – named after the photographer Cecil Beaton – only chewed the plasterwork. It was his way of getting minerals so I allowed it. But my sister has let hers get away with much more. They have eaten everything, even the stuffing out of her sofa! Her house is completely destroyed!

Of all my rabbits, Beaton was by far the most

intelligent. The more nurturing you give and the more sociable you are with any rabbit, the more this develops its brain. Wherever we went, Beaton followed, and whatever we did, he did too. He ate, slept and walked with us. Whenever I made a light salad for my husband, Beaton would jump on the table and start eating it! He obviously thought I had made it for him and seeing them fight over the salad bowl was terribly funny. When we went to bed, Beaton would come up too and fall asleep under our bed, but he was so noisy. At first we couldn't work out what this inhuman sound was – we could hear it above the volume of the TV – but then we realised it was Beaton snoring. From then on we had to wear earplugs!

Since Beaton died three years ago, I haven't replaced him because my lifestyle has changed so much. After *I'm a Celebrity, Get Me Out of Here!* I toured with *Calamity Jane* and I'll be touring with a rock band for a year so I am rarely home. I did consider getting another rabbit and taking it with me, but it would be really difficult and unfair. Rabbits like being in their own environment, surrounded by familiar smells.

I would love to have two rabbits together and in many ways I think it is preferable. I know other people think they are socially better alone and there's also the risk that two won't get on, even if they are the same sex and they are both neutered, so I have mixed feelings. I definitely wouldn't get a guinea pig, though. I know the combination can work but I wouldn't want one.

45

My husband has grown to like rabbits because he has seen how bright they are and what pleasure they bring. But that's only because of all the hard work I have put into teaching them. Teaching them is a journey but, once the path has been plotted, it's there. I have never litter-trained them, though. In that respect girls seem to be easier. Boys are very territorial and spray whenever and wherever they feel the urge. Instead, I've learned to mop up every morning! Beaton was by far the worst of the boys – he marked all the time. He was so enamoured with my husband, he would regularly spray urine all over his back. I was constantly sneaking his shirts into the laundry without explaining why, or wiping it off when he left the house, hoping he wouldn't notice! It helps to castrate them, even though I have never castrated 'my boys'. But in future I think I will!

Beaton also had a fetish for bits of material – he thought they were bits of nooky. So, whenever he escaped into the garden, instead of searching through seven acres, I just waved a towel or piece of fabric in the air. It sent him into a frenzy of desire and he would come running! I could lead him anywhere and he would do exactly as he was told!

Rabbits are at their most active in the morning and every morning at 5 a.m. we would be woken up by Beaton running around the house at a fantastic speed, then every so often we would hear a 'doink'. We would lie in bed and know exactly where he was in the house by the noise he made every time he hit a piece of

furniture! I have always let my rabbits have the run of the house. They weren't born to live in hutches. They are sociable creatures and love to interact, and I want them to enjoy a long and happy life.

I have a stable yard where Beaton played which is by the pavement so people were always looking in when they walked past. One morning I heard a little boy telling Beaton what lessons he would be having at school that day and what he would be eating for break and lunch. He did the same every morning and on the way home he would tell Beaton what sort of day he'd had and what homework he'd been given, and Beaton would just sit there listening! It was so sweet. Beaton was like his little friend.

I have always talked to my rabbits and they would communicate with me too. If I got up early to do some work, Beaton would come into my office and start nudging my neck for attention. If I was busy, I would have to throw him out and close the door, which infuriated him so he would start scratching the door until I let him back in.

I have never had any other pets but I did consider getting a dog to take on walks as a companion. My rabbits have replaced all my maternal instincts. I treat them with the uttermost tenderness, like I would a baby. It's probably not right but the way I feel about rabbits is what I should be feeling towards a human baby! I love their smell and beautiful vulnerability. They are my world and I am theirs!

What a Rabbit Needs

Before bringing bunny home, make sure you are fully prepared. The biggest outlay and most important consideration is, of course, accommodation, and it is important that you have an awareness of what requirements a rabbit has in this respect. It is essential that you provide the right food for your rabbit to ensure that it remains healthy. Grooming is also key to your rabbit's general well-being and you must make sure that it is vaccinated as soon as possible against VHD and Myxomatosis, and that you stay up-to-date with all vaccinations.

ACCOMMODATION

In order to understand what a domesticated rabbit needs in terms of accommodation, we need to look at how rabbits live in the wild.

Wild rabbits live in warrens, made up of a sophisticated network of underground tunnels – or burrows – with numerous entry and exit points. Each tunnel measures about 15cm in diameter, which is large enough for them to get through (wild rabbits are smaller than the average domestic rabbits), but too small for larger predators to enter the warren. The main tunnels lead to large dens where the rabbits sleep and breed. When a doe becomes pregnant, she will prepare a new nesting den where she can give birth to her young and nurse them until they are old enough to join the main colony. Undisturbed, warrens remain in constant use and are regularly extended to accommodate new generations and prevent overcrowding.

There are several things we can learn from this description of rabbits in the wild: rabbits need to be protected from predators; they need their privacy and their accommodation should be split into separate areas; and they need plenty of room for exercise. So what does that mean for you as a rabbit-keeper?

Unless you are intending to keep a house rabbit, which is discussed in more detail in Chapter 8, you will need to provide suitable outdoor accommodation. This will mean that you will have to buy or make a rabbit hutch and, if possible, create a secure area where it can run around.

HUTCHES

The size of hutch is determined by how large you expect your rabbit to be when fully grown. Of course, you may not always be able to predict this, but if you know the breed or have seen the rabbit's parents, you can at least make an educated guess. Bear in mind, though, if the hutch is too small for the adult rabbit, you will have to find a bigger one – it is cruel to keep animals in spaces that are too small for them. Not only will your rabbit develop skeletal problems, but it will also become bored, which will have an adverse effect on its personality.

The hutch should be high enough for the adult rabbit to stand on its hind legs without knocking its head on the ceiling. It should be wide enough for it to be able to perform several hops, and deep enough for it to lie outstretched without touching the sides. Rabbits are active little creatures, so the more space your rabbit has, the happier it will be. Furthermore, the more room a rabbit has, the more opportunity it will have for exercise, and it will be less prone to obesity. Finally, you should remember that small areas are quickly covered with the spread of urine and droppings, which is unhealthy for your rabbit and unpleasant for you.

Like wild rabbits, domestic rabbits should have separate areas for separate activities. A standard hutch, therefore, should have at least two interconnecting rooms with two separate doors: a larger room for living, playing and feeding, with a strong mesh-fronted door to let in air and light; and a smaller side room with a solid door where your rabbit can sleep, breed its young or retire to if it is afraid or feeling unwell. Although far from emulating their natural habitat, this goes some way towards replicating the environment to which they are naturally suited. Even if they have the privilege of being able to run around the house or the rabbit run all day, they should never be made to feel imprisoned.

Rabbits are natural prey, so it is imperative that their hutch is strong and predator-proof. Ideally, therefore, the hutch should be supported on legs or propped up safely on bricks to stop predators trying to force their way in. Alternatively, you could put the hutch on a sturdy table or shelf, as it must be kept off the floor. There are other good reasons for raising hutches off the ground, namely to keep it well ventilated in the hot summer months and in winter, when it rains, it will ensure that the floor does not become cold and damp. It will also prevent all manner of creepy-crawlies from entering – some of which can be quite harmful to your rabbit's health. Although the better of the ready-made hutches are good, there is room for improvement, so it is advisable to get padlocks – the little wooden latches are not sufficient and are actually quite easy for foxes to open.

Rabbits are also prey to predators from above, and so are instinctively afraid of unfamiliar – or even familiar – sights above them. For this reason, hutches should have a good solid roof, sloped to allow water to run off, and covered with waterproof material to keep them dry.

The floor should also be solid, rather than mesh which is draughty and painful underfoot. It is both practical and hygienic to line the floor of the hutch with newspaper – it makes cleaning out easy, and it's cheap! The hutch should contain a generous quantity of good-quality hay or straw. Both are relatively inexpensive and both provide adequate warmth and comfort, but, as hay is cheaper, it is more popular – as it also constitutes part of their staple diet, it needs to be topped up regularly. Whichever you choose for your rabbit hutch, I'm afraid the rule of thumb is that the more expensive it is the better. Cheaper hay contains more seeds and dust that can irritate the eyes, and cheap straw – such as wheat and oat – is more brittle and can poke their eyes and feet. The best – and the most expensive – is barley straw which is soft and warm.

The main frontage of the hutch should be covered with a sturdy wire mesh. This allows your rabbit to look out, you to look in, and will also provide light and vital ventilation. It is important that the wire is both smooth and strong – chicken wire is not suitable as they will nibble through it in no time. The openings in the mesh should not be too large – certainly no more than 2.5cm wide – to avoid the risk of your rabbit getting one of its limbs caught up in the gap and to stop other animals such as mice from entering.

Other essential items that you will need to include in the hutch are a food bowl, which should be made of earthenware – not plastic, as it is too light and can be easily knocked over, plus rabbits love to chew away at it. Stainless steel gets too hot in the summer and too cold in the winter. Adding a bark-covered log will give them something natural to gnaw at – and hopefully stop them having a go at the hutch itself. Water should be provided in a water bottle attached to the wire mesh, not in a bowl – it will tip over, make the floor wet and is more likely to become contaminated.

You can buy special hay racks that hook on to the wire meshing at the front of the hutch. These offer a better alternative to eating hay that has been placed inside the hutch that will have been trodden on and soiled.

The positioning of your hutch is crucial. If your rabbit is outside, it is exposed to the elements, and you need to have an understanding of what domestic rabbits can and cannot tolerate. Generally speaking, rabbits can tolerate the cold far better than they can tolerate the heat, and temperatures above 80°C can be dangerous for them. You should therefore keep the hutch in a shady place, away from direct sunlight – under a tree perhaps. And while colder temperatures aren't necessarily a problem for rabbits, sudden changes in temperature can be, as can prolonged exposure to cold wind, so make sure that the hutch is in a sheltered position away from strong winds and rain. Dampness too is a problem for rabbits, but if you have a well-ventilated hutch with a wire-mesh front, and have weather-proofed the exterior, it shouldn't be too much of a problem – just be aware of it. Creosoting the outside of the hutch will waterproof it and preserve the wood but *never* creosote the inside as it is poisonous to rabbits. Finally, rabbits like peace and quiet – it is a typical characteristic of prey animals, and they become nervous if there is a lot of commotion nearby. If possible, keep the hutch away from areas where there are likely to be loud noises such as children playing or cars starting up.

A HUTCH-CLEANING SCHEDULE

Rabbits are naturally clean-living creatures, so their accommodation needs to be kept to the same scrupulously clean high standards – especially in the summer when the heat can cause bad odours and infections, introduced by flies and other insects which are attracted to the rabbit droppings and urine. Although they are hygienic animals, in captivity you will have to do the housework for them! And get into the habit of daily and weekly cleaning.

The more time rabbits spend in their hutch, the more it will need to be cleaned out. If the rabbit is in permanent residence, you should remove any rabbit droppings every few days – it's amazing how quickly they accumulate. The food dish should always be clean and dry, and the water bottle should be washed in soapy water and then thoroughly rinsed before being refilled with clean fresh water. You should also check and top up the hay or straw. Generally speaking, rabbits are creatures of habit and will urinate and defecate in the same place. Rarely do they mess in the nesting area, but, if they do, be sure to remove any soiled or wet bedding and replace it with fresh.

On a weekly basis, you should clean out the hutch thoroughly. Remove all the bedding and newspaper, then brush it all out and start again. Three or four times a year, you should wash the insides with a solution of one part bleach to ten parts water. Always ensure the hutch is thoroughly dry before refilling it with bedding. In winter, dry it indoors.

It is particularly important that you should thoroughly disinfect a hutch before a new rabbit moves in, especially if the previous occupant has died of any kind of illness – to prevent the infection spreading to your new rabbit.

RABBIT RUNS

Rabbits, like humans, will derive no pleasure from being cooped up all day, and it is essential for their general well-being that they should be allowed time to run around and exercise. Even domestic rabbits need a natural environment. If you have the time to supervise your pet while it is doing this, all well and good; but most of us do not, so a simple rabbit run is an excellent way of making sure it gets all the exercise it needs.

A rabbit run is an enclosed area that gives your pet a larger space and so more opportunities to move around than it would have in its hutch alone. I would advise that you consider buying or making a portable rabbit run, so it can be moved to a new area every few days – this prevents your rabbit overusing the same space, which will quickly become dirty and unhygienic (although droppings do fertilise the ground). If you are lucky enough to have an area of lawn, your rabbit can benefit from fresh grass.

The rabbit run should be constructed of a solid wooden frame and covered with a strong, good-quality wire mesh. Ideally, there should also be a wire-mesh floor – not only to stop your rabbit burrowing out, but also to stop other predators burrowing in – but if your rabbit is there for long periods of time it can end up with sore hocks. If possible, therefore, press it firmly into the ground to allow the grass to act as soft flooring. You should always place the rabbit run where there is plenty of shade – we have already seen that strong sunlight and overheating can be dangerous for rabbits – and also make sure there is plenty of fresh water.

If your run is big enough, it is a good idea to supply a little hiding house for your pet. Rabbits get easily scared, so will appreciate somewhere to hide away. And don't be tempted to leave your rabbit in its run all day while you are out. Although predators probably won't be able to get in, this will not necessarily stop them trying. This can be very distressing for your rabbit, and it is not inconceivable that a bad shock will scare it to death …

Again, if you have enough room in your rabbit run, it is a good idea to provide a few toys and obstacles. They needn't be anything extravagant or expensive, but anything it can hop over, hide under or bite on will make it happy. A log to jump over, an upturned flowerpot, a gnawing block and ball are all good stimulants.

FEEDING

Rabbits love to eat. They are famous for it! Wild rabbits are known for the detrimental effects they have on crops – in 1937, a select committee of the House of Lords suggested that 'the rabbit has seldom been killed which, on sale, did not owe somebody several shillings as a result of its depredations'.

Rabbits are vegetarian and, whether domesticated or in the wild, their staple food is grass. This is presented to domestic rabbits in the form of hay, and you should not underestimate its importance to your pet. Even rabbits that are being fed on so-called 'complete' rabbit foods – which we will discuss in a minute – should be given a good quantity of hay. It is high in fibre, which is essential for a rabbit's digestive system, and low in fat, starch and sugar. Importantly, it also has an abrasive action on the teeth – rabbits need to be chewing for a good few hours a day to wear down their teeth, which are constantly growing. The best hay is young and has a slight green colour– old hay will have lost most of its nutritional value. It should smell fresh, and not be dry and dusty. Also, strange as this may seem, rabbits become bored if they don't have something to nibble at, so hay is the perfect thing for diverting their attention! No matter what else you feed your rabbit, you need to make sure it has a plentiful supply.

But rabbits cannot live on hay alone. Like humans, they need a balanced diet. This should consist of proteins for growth, carbohydrates and fats for energy, fibre to aid digestion plus essential minerals and vitamins. The healthiest, most natural source of fibre is a selection of fresh vegetables, leafy greens and grass but, as this can be time-consuming to prepare, most rabbit owners use commercially produced rabbit foods and supplement these with fresh vegetables.

Commercial rabbit foods come as either mixes or pellets. The mixes may look more appealing to us humans, but there are disadvantages to using them. Rabbits, believe it or not, can be rather fussy eaters. As a result of this, sometimes they only eat certain ingredients in the rabbit mix and so do not get the benefit of a balanced diet. If you encounter this problem, I would recommend you switch to rabbit pellets. These are little nuggets of food which all have the same make-up. They may not look quite as appetising to you and me, but they do get round the problem of selective eating and so ensure that your rabbit is getting all the nutrients it needs.

Alongside the commercial rabbit foods, you should also give your rabbit a variety of fresh leaves and vegetables. The following are the most readily available and are good for them:

Brussels sprouts
Broccoli
Cabbage
Carrots and carrot tops
Celery
Chicory
Parsley
Parsnips
Peas

Have a look at the Appendix (page 207) for a list of some more delicious rabbit snacks. Contrary to popular belief, lettuce is not especially good for rabbits – it can even have a rather soporific effect. There are also certain leaves and plants that are poisonous for rabbits – see the Appendix for a list of these.

Many owners like to spoil their rabbits by giving them sweet treats. I would strongly advise against this. Too many sugars and starches can give your rabbit intestinal problems that can make them very ill – they can even be fatal. If you want to treat your rabbit, give it a tasty apple core instead. It will love you all the more for it!

Rabbits need plenty of water, so do make sure your pet has a constant supply. You may find that rabbits that eat more greens tend to drink less water; this is because they are getting a certain amount from the leaves. Some people put mineral drops in the water; personally I think it is also a good idea to attach a mineral lick to the mesh of the rabbit's hutch – either will ensure it is getting all the vitamins and minerals it needs.

So now you know *what* to feed your rabbit, the next question is, how much? As we have already learned, rabbits *really* like to eat. In the wild this is not a problem – wild rabbits are much more active than the domesticated variety, so they actually need more food. However, obesity can be a real problem with domestic rabbits, so, if you are preparing your own feed, be sure to get the balances right if you want them to live a long and healthy life.

Overfeeding is less of an issue with baby rabbits who, once they are weaned, can eat as much as they like up until their rate of growth slows down. This normally happens between four and six months. After that, the rule of thumb is that a rabbit should eat four per cent of its body weight each day but, as each rabbit's metabolism is different, keep a close eye on its weight. If in doubt, ask your vet for advice.

One final tip: don't be surprised if you see your rabbit eating its own droppings – this is perfectly normal!

VACCINATIONS

Rabbits need to be vaccinated against life-threatening diseases: viral haemorrhagic disease (VHD) and myxomatosis. The process of vaccination stimulates the rabbit's immune system and teaches it to recognise these diseases, and so produce antibodies to combat them. Both these diseases are very virulent, and every responsible rabbit owner should make sure that their pets are vaccinated against them.

VHD

Any rabbit, wild or domesticated, over the age of six weeks is susceptible to the deadly VHD. It does not affect humans, but it can be carried by humans in clothing and footwear, as well as being transported by birds and insects, which is why it spreads so quickly. It can also be passed from rabbit to rabbit, through saliva and nasal secretions. The disease kills all infected rabbits by attacking the liver and causing severe bleeding. The infected animals die very quickly, and there is no cure. The only way of preventing VHD is by vaccination.

Baby rabbits up to six weeks are resistant, so most are first vaccinated against VHD at the age of ten weeks, and will require a booster vaccination at least once a year, twice if they are kept outside or if there is an outbreak. In some high-risk situations, they are vaccinated earlier than six weeks and require a second dose, but your vet will be able to advise you on this.

MYXOMATOSIS

Myxomatosis is the most high-profile and most prevalent rabbit disease, affecting both wild and domesticated rabbits. It is spread by fleas and other blood-sucking insects, and, although some rabbits infected with the virus will recover with expert medical attention, the vast majority will die unless they are protected. Those that do survive may be horrifically disfigured.

Rabbits must be vaccinated from the age of six weeks and will require a booster vaccination every year, more frequently if they are in a high-risk area. Most vets will notify you if there is an outbreak.

GROOMING

Rabbits are fastidiously clean. They are constantly grooming themselves and each other and, with a few exceptions, generally keep themselves in pretty good shape. Nevertheless, it is a good idea for you to consider giving them a bit of a helping hand.

Grooming is important for a number of reasons. Firstly, brushing your rabbit's coat enables you to remove any loose and matted hair. It also gives you the opportunity to examine your rabbit close up, and it is a wonderful opportunity for you to have a bonding session with your pet.

How often you groom will depend on what fur-type your rabbit is. Long-haired varieties such as the Angora will require much more grooming – up to once a day – than the short-haired varieties, which don't need grooming more than once a week, if at all. You will need to get yourself a good-quality grooming brush and brush your rabbit very gently – their skins are really quite sensitive and, if you brush them too vigorously, you will put them off the process for life.

Rabbits with longer fur or digestive problems are prone to having droppings caked around the anal area. This should be cleaned regularly, especially in the summer, as it can put the rabbit at risk of a very unpleasant condition called flystrike. This occurs when flies lay eggs on the dirty fur and they hatch into maggots. To avoid this, you should examine the area carefully every day. If it does need cleaning, start by brushing out any dried droppings as far as possible, then wash gently around the area until it is clean.

There are certain things you should look out for as you are grooming:

PARASITES

When you are brushing your rabbit, keep a lookout for fleas and ticks. Fleas can be difficult to spot, but their faeces can be seen as small, dark specks on the neck, the back and the behind of the rabbit. Several species of flea can be found on rabbits, including those that infest dog and cat fur, and they can cause a great deal of irritation and discomfort. Your vet will be able to recommend a special powder that will rid your rabbit of them, but you need to be aware that, if your rabbit is infected with fleas, they may be breeding in the hutch itself. The hutch should therefore be cleaned thoroughly and sprayed with a special product, such as Xenex Ultra, that will keep the larvae away for several months – again, your vet will be able to advise you about this.

Ticks appear as dark round protrusions. Don't try and pull them off. You can smear them with a little Vaseline, which will suffocate them, or you can ask your vet to recommend a special spray or powder to get rid of them.

LUMPS AND SORES

As you brush your pet, keep an eye out for any unfamiliar lumps or sores on its body. These can be a sign of parasite or bacterial infection, and should be referred to your vet.

TOENAIL CLIPPING

Rabbits' toenails – like those of humans – are always growing. Wild rabbits automatically keep their nails trimmed by constantly burrowing and digging for food. With regular exercise and access to hard areas, domestic rabbits rarely have a problem, but, if their nails are allowed to grow too long, it can become quite uncomfortable for them and cause unintentional harm to others. Part of your grooming process, therefore, should include keeping an eye on growth and, if necessary, toenail clipping.

You won't need to clip your rabbit's toenails every time you groom it but, just for the record, if the nail extends beyond the fur of the rabbit's foot, it's too long and will need to be clipped. If you're not sure, ask a vet and, while you're at it, you could even ask them to do it for you, especially if you've not done it before. It's a fairly straightforward process that you can do yourself but you will need to buy special guillotine-type nail clippers which are available from pet shops and make the process much easier. If you look closely at the nail, you will see a vein extending down the centre from the foot. Make sure you do not clip across this vein, as that will make the toenail bleed.

Bear in mind that rabbits do not much like having their toenails clipped and will struggle, so it will be easier if you draft in a helper to hold your rabbit while you do it.

Nick Ferrari

Boston and Lucy

Having moved through the ranks from reporter to Editor of the major red-top tabloids, Nick then moved to New York as VP of News and Programming at Fox TV. On returning to England, he was made Director of Programmes at Live TV but before long he moved into radio where he gained wider recognition and received the highly prestigious and coveted Commercial Radio Presenter of the Year Award in recognition of his ability to amuse his listeners with his controversial views of the news which are aired each morning on LBC 97.3FM. Away from the heated debates, he relaxes by sailing.

Our boys wanted a rabbit because one of their friends at school had one and, of course, we let them. It is the sort of thing parents often do for their children, and what mine did for me when I was a child.

We got two rabbits, but I did not know much about keeping them, even though I had had rabbits as a child, so we asked the pet-shop staff for advice about feeding and care in general. They also told us what size hutch and run we should have and what the daily routine would involve, all of which was very useful. Our vet was very good too. He suggested having an area with a hard surface so they could wear down their nails to keep them trim, and advised us about any jabs they needed to prevent diseases. Apart from that, however, I learned the rest as I went along. I have no idea what breed they were – only that one was a male and the other a female!

We were going to get them neutered, but the boys wanted them to have babies. Baby rabbits are so cute, so we agreed to let them have one go first before we had them done. Sadly, unlike most rabbits, Boston must have been firing blanks! No matter how hard he tried – and God knows he tried enough and got it down to a fine art – nothing ever happened, so we didn't need to get them neutered after all. I know it is advisable but, luckily, they were never temperamental. Our kids and their friends would play happily with them and they never reacted badly. They were sensational!

Then the boys grew up and, being typical teenagers, got more interested in cars and girls, and lost interest in the rabbits. So I inherited the responsibility of looking after Boston and Lucy, but I really did not mind at all. In fact, I can honestly say I loved it.

My wife is not particularly interested in animals and feels differently, but I grew up in the country surrounded by animals and we always had pets. My parents owned a beautiful old mill house in Farningham, Kent, with a smallholding where they kept ponies, donkeys, ducks, chickens and a rare breed of sheep, which my father bred as a hobby. I really enjoyed working with them and being with animals generally, so I genuinely loved looking after the rabbits. I dreaded the day anything happened to them, and each Christmas I would look at them and wonder if they would make it through to the next one.

Then, tragically, Boston died of a suspected heart attack three years ago. He was seven, so he lived to a good age. He was a gorgeous mink grey colour, not a common or garden type, so he probably was not as tough as Lucy, who is now ten years old. She is a more common black-and-white breed, and still going strong.

Lucy and Boston had a summer residence and a winter residence. In the summer, they had a great big hutch and large run in the garden. In the winter, they lived in the utility room, where they had a smaller hutch and the run of the room, which we could lock so they could not get out – and the cat and dog could not get in. Although all the animals seemed to get on well together, I would never leave the rabbits alone with our other pets, especially the cat. Cats are basically feral and I worried that, if one of the rabbits upset our tabby, she would have them for dinner. That would really break my heart.

Animals bring so much pleasure – and best of all they do not answer back! Rabbits are so easy to keep and relatively cheap to run. They are also very clean and, if they should get caught short on the way to the litter tray, it is never messy. We were lucky because we didn't have to litter-train our rabbits and, apart from one exception, there has never been an accident. When they needed to go, they just went into the hutch and did it!

There are of course disadvantages to having rabbits, as there are with any other pet. They are not as responsive as cats and dogs – mine would rarely come when called, only when they saw food – and they will eat through anything. I do not know what it is about them but they will strip a power cable better than any electrician can! Boston was by far the worst, but between them they have eaten through numerous TV cables and wires!

When Boston died, I was worried that Lucy would be lonely and need psychological help but, oddly, she seems happier now she is on her own. Every time I go to feed her and change her bedding or give her new straw and water, she is so genuinely grateful, so I really do not mind doing anything for her. I suppose the very nature of her being alone means she is getting more attention so she didn't need any bereavement counselling! Now I dread the day I go down to feed Lucy and there is no rustling in the hutch, but I know that one day soon she will join Boston in rabbit heaven.

3

Rabbits and Your Family

So you've chosen your rabbit and you've got everything it needs. Now it's time to look at how to make sure it really is part of the family. After all, that's what we all want from a pet, isn't it? Like all relationships, however, it requires a bit of work, and that starts with integrating your pet into your family.

HANDLING YOUR RABBIT

Rabbits respond extremely well to handling and affection, so the more a rabbit is handled the better. It builds up mutual trust and confidence between owner and pet, and will initiate a bond that will make the relationship more fulfilling for everyone. But it is very important that you learn how to handle your rabbit in the correct way. At best, incorrect handling is uncomfortable and is likely to make the rabbit unwilling to continue; at worst it can actually cause damage to its internal organs, which naturally is to be avoided at all costs.

Before attempting to pick up your bunny, you need to earn its trust, which is immediately easier to do with a baby rabbit than with an adult. Start off simply by spending time together. Put yourself at its level, either by placing the rabbit on a table, or by getting down on the floor. As already mentioned, rabbits are prey to larger predators, so anything coming at them from above will automatically make them nervous. Gently stroke your rabbit and talk softly to it for a short period of time, and repeat this over a few days. Pay careful attention to its body language: if it seems relaxed, you're heading in the right direction. You want your rabbit to come to you, so if it starts putting its paw on your hand or brushing up against you, you are ready to go to the next stage.

Place one hand underneath the rabbit's chest for support, then place the other around its rump. Using the hand that is underneath the rabbit, lift upwards, using the other hand to support the weight. Firmly but gently, bring the rabbit towards you then, with its head pointing towards the back of your elbow and still supporting from the rump, move your arm out from underneath. If your rabbit starts to struggle, it can easily slip off, so, hold it a little more firmly. If it continues, carefully put it down and try again.

Alternatively, support it under the hind legs with one hand and let it rest its forelegs on your shoulder. If they should struggle while you are holding them in this way, they are less likely to fall. I prefer this way, partly because they can be held more securely, but also because babies in particular can take comfort from hearing your heartbeat and feeling the warmth of your body.

As you gradually increase the amount of time you spend holding your rabbit, both you and it will become more accustomed to the process. Stroke your rabbit calmly and reassuringly and you will find it will become very relaxed.

If you have trouble picking up your rabbit, don't panic. There are perfectly good reasons why this might be the case: if it's a rescue animal, for example, it may have been poorly treated in the past and will therefore be afraid of being held by humans. It just means that you will have to be a little more patient and invest a little more time bonding before your pet allows you to pick him or her up. Sometimes, though, you really need to pick up your rabbit, for example, when cleaning out the hutch or putting it in a run. If it remains nervous, it is acceptable to pick it up by the scruff, as you may have seen other people do. Rabbits don't particularly like this, and I have never done this myself, but it will not cause them any harm provided it is done properly: you must make sure you support their rump as you do it. On no account – no matter how many times you have seen your favourite magician do it! – should a rabbit be picked up by its ears. It can be very extremely painful and will put any hard bonding work several steps back in one go.

A final word of advice about handling your rabbit. Try to avoid putting it on its back – it frightens them terribly. Just because it *looks* relaxed, it doesn't mean it is. Often rabbits on their backs lie still out of sheer fear.

INTRODUCING CHILDREN TO RABBITS

You only have to see how much pleasure children get from going to the zoo to know how much they love animals. The problem is that, when a child wants an animal, parents often say yes in a moment of weakness without thinking their decision through properly. They forget that they too will have a role in caring for the pet, which to young children is really no more than a fluffy toy. A few minutes of patting is a long way from the reality of owning a pet for several years.

Like toys, it would help if pets came with a warning – Not Suitable for Children Under the Age of Seven – or even a rating like films, only in this case to protect the pet, not the child, from harmful influences. On that basis, rabbits would definitely be rated PG, with perhaps a 'Handle With Care' tag attached for good measure.

That warning aside, rabbits are actually an ideal pet for children. More robust and sociable than mice and hamsters, yet less of a tie than cats and dogs, they are also a lot of fun for adults, should they end up with the responsibility of looking after them full-time. No wonder they have cornered the small-pet market. With parental guidance, there is no reason why children should not be allowed to have a rabbit. In fact, research has shown that pets should be positively encouraged for children. Looking after a pet can help with a child's self-esteem and self-confidence. Having a good relationship with a pet can help children learn how to have positive and trusting relationships with other people. It can also help a child develop their non-verbal communication skills, as well as encouraging them to be kinder, less selfish and more sympathetic. Children often talk to their pets, as they do to their soft toys, and so a pet in the family can be a safe recipient of private thoughts. They help children learn important life lessons too – reproduction, birth, illness and death being just a few. Learning to care for animals helps children understand what is responsible behaviour and teaches them respect for living things. Add comfort, love and affection into the mix, and it is clear that there are many advantages to a child having a pet. Those brought up with animals develop into more thoughtful, caring adults.

However, it is unreasonable to expect a child to act like a responsible adult. Let's face it: they can't even tidy their bedrooms or do their homework without being nagged, so why should we expect them to clean out the hutch, for example? This is why it is so important for parents to get involved. By allowing children the pleasures of playing with their rabbit, they will develop a close friendship and, once that has been established, they will automatically want to do everything for them and begin to take an active interest in the more practical aspects of their rabbit's life.

Introducing a child to a rabbit for the first time is a crucial moment: it will determine how well the relationship will develop and should always be supervised by an adult who knows how to handle rabbits correctly. Start the bonding process slowly and begin with placing the rabbit on your child's lap so that they can stroke it – a soft cushion on the lap provides a more comfortable surface for the rabbit and, should it struggle, its claws won't accidentally hurt your child. Never hurry the process, and never leave children unsupervised. Repeat this for a few days and then, when both your child and the rabbit seem comfortable, you can let them hold it.

Always make sure your child is relaxed and sitting comfortably. Rabbits are afraid of heights and can sustain injuries from a fall, so it is best if your child is seated on the floor. Before letting a child hold a rabbit, demonstrate how it should be held and explain the importance of getting this right. Teaching by example and explanation is by far the most effective way.

It is important that this first introduction goes smoothly. Held incorrectly, rabbits will struggle and accidentally scratch which, for a child, is scary. It may put them off trying to hold them again. Should this happen, leave it for a few days before making another attempt. Both child and rabbit will be feeling afraid and will need time to recover. Don't rush things.

Make children aware of the fact that rabbits don't react well to loud noises, so if they want to run around and shout, they must do so well away from the rabbit's quarters. They must also understand that rabbits are not like dogs – always eager to play. They need periods of rest and children should learn to respect that. Most children enjoy feeding time with their rabbit, and there is no reason why they shouldn't be involved – it helps teach them about the responsibility involved in caring for a pet. However, they need to be taught that, if they want to see the rabbit eat, they must sit very quietly – rabbits become nervous if there is too much activity around them – and on no account should they try to stroke or pick up the rabbit while it is trying to eat.

INTRODUCING YOUR RABBIT TO OTHER PETS

As we have already learned, rabbits are prey animals. The pets that they are most likely to come into contact with – cats and dogs – are predatory animals. This does not mean that they have to be kept apart – rabbits are sociable animals, and can live very happily alongside other pets if you go about it the right way – but there are certain issues you need to be aware of.

Generally speaking, mature dogs and cats are easier to introduce to rabbits than overaffectionate and playful young ones. If they have been neutered or spayed, so much the better – it tends to reduce any aggressive instincts they may have. Above all, common sense is the key – you will be able to tell if your pets are getting on or not by paying close attention to their behaviour.

Cats and dogs are not the only animals to which you may want to introduce your pet rabbit. Rabbits love company and so will thrive in the presence of other rabbits, but again only if you go about it the right way. Rabbits and guinea pigs can also be great friends and are often chosen as hutch companions, but again you do need to be aware of certain issues concerning the pairing of these two species, as is discussed below.

RABBITS AND DOGS

As a rule, retrievers or terriers are unlikely to get on well with rabbits. Retrievers do just what their name suggests – retrieve prey – and terriers have been bred for hundreds of years to hunt all manner of prey, including rabbits – but there are exceptions to every rule. For example, our Labrador adores our cats, Patchy Petra the rabbit and Sherman the guinea pig. Equally, other, more docile breeds may react badly to a rabbit. Bear in mind that puppies can be very distressing for rabbits, even if they themselves think they are just being playful! While a puppy might love chasing a rabbit around, the rabbit will hate it.

If a rabbit is to be introduced into a family where there is already a dog, make sure that the dog is already well trained.

When introducing the two animals, make sure that the rabbit is in an environment where it feels safe and secure – its hutch is probably the best place. Bring your dog to the hutch, let the two animals observe each other for a few minutes, then take the dog away. Don't worry if your rabbit retires to hide in its nest box – it is natural for it to be scared of a dog. Gradually, as the two animals become more familiar with each other, your rabbit will become braver. Repeat this introductory process over a few days, until you feel that the rabbit is showing signs of interest in and familiarity with the dog, and you are sure that your dog is not looking at the rabbit as though it is lunch.

When they have reached this stage, take your rabbit out of its hutch and introduce it nose-to-nose with the dog. Keep a close eye on your rabbit: if it seems scared, try again another day. If your dog starts misbehaving, be very firm and take it away; if all goes well, you have effected a successful introduction. Don't make the mistake, however, of assuming that, just because your dog and your rabbit get along when you are there, they can be left alone together. No matter how good their intentions, some dogs just can't resist chasing a rabbit!

RABBITS AND CATS

Cats cohabit far more easily with rabbits than dogs do. If anything, cats are sometimes more afraid of rabbits than the other way round. That said, some cats can behave aggressively towards a rabbit even if it is generally docile with you. Be particularly wary of cats that have a habit of bringing home dead mice or birds – it shows a hunter-gatherer streak and could indicate a more hostile attitude towards rabbits too.

Start by making sure that your cat's claws are well trimmed. Bring your cat to the rabbit's hutch and watch how they react to each other: if the cat hisses and runs away, or if the rabbit retires to its nest, try again another day. Both cats and rabbits are naturally rather inquisitive, so their curiosity will get the better of them, and, when this happens, take the rabbit from the hutch and introduce them face-to-face. Pay careful attention to your cat: if it starts to stalk your rabbit, never leave them alone. After a while, and as both are exceptionally clean, you may find that your rabbit and your cat may even start to groom each other, lie down together and generally be very comfortable in each other's company. If they reach this stage, it is safe to leave them alone; otherwise, always supervise any time they spend together.

RABBITS AND OTHER RABBITS

Don't automatically assume that a new rabbit will instantly get on with another rabbit that is already part of the family. They are naturally territorial, and are wary of other, unfamiliar rabbits coming on to their patch. Many believe that the best combination – by which I mean the combination least likely to lead to aggression between the two – is a male and a female. Unless you are intending to breed them (see Chapter 7), ensure that both are neutered, as this makes them more docile. If only one or the other has been done, there is a risk of sexual attentions from one, leading to aggression from the other. Although the male/female coupling generally works best, putting rabbits of the same sex together also works: does can live happily together but un-neutered bucks should be housed separately once they are three months old. Rabbits that come from the same litter tend to get along fine; but, if you are introducing a new rabbit to an existing rabbit, the male/female option is often the best combination.

Unlike introductions with different species, e.g. a cat or a dog, it's best to introduce rabbits on neutral territory, and I have found that the easiest way to do it is to place each rabbit in separate carrying boxes next to each other, so that they can see each other but can't get at each other! The more relaxed they seem to be, the closer together you can place the boxes. When they appear to be perfectly relaxed, let the established rabbit out to have a bit of a sniff around – this is the rabbit you are most likely to have problems with, as it will feel as though its territory is being infringed upon. Keep a close eye on them: if you see any signs of aggression, calmly remove the new rabbit and try again the next day.

The aim is to reach a situation whereby each rabbit seems completely unbothered by the other, even to the extent that they seem to be ignoring each other. If this appears to be the case, it is safe to let them roam free in an area of the house or garden where they can be carefully observed. Again, make sure there are no signs of aggression – if there are, go back to the beginning of the introduction process and start all over again. Don't worry – they will eventually get used to each other and will enjoy life all the more for having a bit of company.

RABBITS AND GUINEA PIGS

This is a common combination; it can also be one of the most problematic. In extreme cases, rabbits have been known to bully guinea pigs; even more unfortunately, it's not always clear that this is the case until the guinea pig has suffered at the hands of its bullying housemate – they can be bitten, starved or even chased to the point of exhaustion. That said, rabbits and guinea pigs *can* live together happily – I know because I have both – but you do need to be vigilant.

It's preferable to introduce rabbits and guinea pigs in an environment where they both have the opportunity to graze – the process of eating, of which they are both inordinately fond, can stop them from paying each other too much attention. Try placing them on a patch of grass in the garden, or on a piece of newspaper in the house, with some tasty greens scattered on it, and make sure you watch them constantly. If the rabbit shows any signs of aggression, remove the guinea pig immediately and try again another day.

If the guinea pig is to be moved into an existing rabbit's hutch, clean it out thoroughly with a mild disinfectant. This removes any traces of territorial urine spraying that the rabbit may have indulged in, and so stop any reflex actions kicking in that will make the rabbit try to defend its territory. Some experts suggest rubbing a little Vicks on to the guinea pig's rear-end fur and under the rabbit's nose: this helps mask any smells that will trigger aggression in your rabbit. Another good precaution is to include a little 'escape box' in the hutch, with an opening just big enough for the guinea pig to enter but too small for the rabbit to follow.

You should also be aware of the fact that rabbits and guinea pigs have different dietary requirements.

DEALING WITH THE LOSS OF A PET

As time goes on, rabbits will become an integral part of the family. We bond with our pets, and that means we feel all the emotions that come with any relationship: we appreciate their companionship, we feel a need to look after them, we worry when they are ill and, of course, we grieve when they die. As your rabbit gets older, therefore, you should prepare yourself for the inevitable.

When our pets become ill, most owners will do anything to make sure they get better. Sometimes, though, the sad fact is that it simply won't happen. Owners are then faced with the difficult decision of letting the pet die naturally, or having it put to sleep. Some people, for reasons I personally don't understand, consider pet euthanasia to be cruel. But the reality is that most domestic animals live much longer than they would in the wild, and it is important for owners to consider whether keeping their pet alive through the wonders of modern medicine is actually improving its quality of life or just prolonging its pain. With rabbits, the questions you need to ask yourself are as follows:

- Is your rabbit enjoying its food, or has it ceased to eat properly?
- Is it active or is it lethargic?
- Is it consistently showing signs of illness?
- Does it have difficulty walking?
- Does it show signs of discomfort when picked up?
- Do the bad days outnumber the good?

The answers to these questions should point you in the direction of the right decision, but, for added comfort, discuss the matter with your vet, who will be able to give you proper, experienced advice. They will be able to predict better than you the long-term effects of keeping your rabbit alive; however, it is your decision, so make sure you fully understand whatever illness your rabbit might be suffering from in order to eliminate any doubts you may have after the event. You should also consider the fact that a natural death is often more distressing for the pet than being put to sleep. Once it is clear that the rabbit is no longer enjoying life, and that veterinary medicine cannot help it any more, many people decide that euthanasia is, in fact, the kindest option after all.

While considering this option, you should also understand what is involved. The process of putting a rabbit to sleep is perfectly humane and does not cause the animal any pain. It is injected with a strong anaesthetic solution, so it feels as if it is simply falling asleep. Once the animal is under, its breathing will stop.

If you do decide to have your pet put to sleep, the chances are that you will enter a perfectly natural period of mourning – as indeed you will if your rabbit dies naturally. Although a painful thought, making a decision as to what to do with the pet's body can sometimes help you come to terms with the death. If the rabbit is put to sleep at the vet's, many owners elect to say goodbye there and leave the body for them to dispose of. Most surgeries now arrange for the pets to be cremated, which is deemed to be the most acceptable way of doing things, but check with your own individual surgery as to what arrangements it can make.

Some people prefer a home burial, feeling that the presence of their pet will be a source of comfort for them. This is fine; indeed the presence of the grave nearby can be a focus for the owner's grief, helping them to cope with the grieving process more effectively. Others might decide to have their pet cremated first and then bury the ashes or place them in a casket. If you decide against these options, do make sure that you dig a deep burial hole

– about 1 metre – to stop the body becoming prey to scavengers. A heavy stone or slab placed over the top will help too. There is an urban myth about a family whose dog brought in their neighbour's rabbit, stone dead. Horrified, the family washed it clean and put it back in its hutch under the cover of night, hoping that the owners would believe it had died in its sleep. A few days later, over the garden fence, the owner of the rabbit told a member of the family, 'The strangest thing happened. We buried our pet rabbit last Thursday and the following day it reappeared in its hutch!' Who knows if it really happened, but if it happened to you it wouldn't be funny – so make sure you dig deep.

The third option is taking your pet to a pet cemetery. These are becoming more and more popular, and offer the advantage of a permanent burial place for your pet, so you can still visit even when you move house. There are a few things you should check out about a pet cemetery before you decide whether or not to use it:

- How much does it cost?
- Do you have to pay a yearly maintenance fee?
- Are the graves permanent, or do they get reused after a few years have passed?
- Is the cemetery built on consecrated ground, or is there a risk that the land will be sold and used for something else?

Once you have said goodbye to your rabbit, you need to come to terms with your loss. Don't underestimate the feelings of loss that the death of a pet can engender. Many people are tempted to shrug it off as if it is not a serious thing, but it is – so you will almost certainly go through the same grieving process as you might experience when you have to come to terms with the loss of a person. This includes disbelief, anger, guilt and sadness. You need to overcome all these feelings before you can finally accept that your pet has passed on – and that takes time.

Chris Tarrant OBE

Thumper and Me

Chris Tarrant OBE started his award-winning TV career as a newsreader for ATV Birmingham which led to him becoming a household name as producer and presenter of the now cult children's show *TISWAS* and adult late-night show *OTT*. From the Midlands he moved to London to host Capital Radio's breakfast show where he

remained for a record 17 years and he has hosted numerous TV shows including *Tarrant on TV* and the multiple-award-winning game show *Who Wants to be a Millionaire?*.

As a little boy, my experiences of pets were pretty disastrous. In fact, they were totally disastrous. I seem to remember finding a never-ending procession of upside-down goldfish in the mornings before school. Some of them didn't last more than a few days, and at least one was dead on arrival from the pet shop! Each passing goldfish was mourned deeply for a matter of minutes and then buried with full ceremony before leaving for school, his or her grave marked with a little wooden cross.

Then there was Goldie the hamster, who I got for my birthday in October and had great fun with for several weeks until she decided to hibernate – or so I thought. In spite of regular cleaning out and removal of bedding, the cage seemed to get smellier and smellier until eventually we realised that Goldie wasn't asleep at all – she'd been dead for weeks!

And I can't not mention Digger the budgie – there was nothing wrong with him. He was a great pet. He lasted two or three years, learned to talk and everything. It was only the manner of his burial that I wasn't so keen on. Fed up with all the little graves that foxes and dogs kept digging up at the end of our garden, my dad –

normally a very kind, caring man – decided to cremate Digger instead by throwing his little stiff budgie body on the fire. Horrors! No wonder I've grown up so peculiar.

There were white mice, frogs, rats, a slow worm or two and a cat called The Hulk who was so aggressive I gave it away to another boy I didn't like much. But by far the most aggressive of all was Thumper the Rabbit. Thumper by name, thumper by nature! He was a big black-and-white bunny that my mum's mum Nanny Cox had bought from a pet shop in Reading. She brought it home one evening and, sitting on her lap contentedly as she stroked its big, floppy ears, it seemed the perfect pet. 'Let me have a stroke, Nanny,' I asked happily and she passed it across.

Well, on switching to my lap, Thumper was a rabbit transformed. It flew at me with its claws extended, scratched me savagely on the leg (I was only wearing shorts!) and sank its teeth deeply into my arm. I squealed in real pain and burst into floods of tears. 'What did you do to it?' asked my mum.

'Nothing,' I protested through sobs.

'Well give it to me,' she said, outraged, and took it from me only to get a savage display of the same, vicious behaviour, ending in a really nasty bite on the shoulder.

Nanny took the raging bunny from us very nervously, fully expecting another attack, at which point, to all our amazement, Thumper stopped thumping and sat back calmly again on her lap, allowing his ears to be fondled and even his whiskers to be stroked.

When my dad came in from work, Thumper seemed to have calmed down again and we all agreed he was a really good-looking pet as he sat there happily on Nanny's lap looking positively at peace. At peace, that is, until Dad, as Master of the House, decided to give the amiable little fellow a gentle welcoming stroke. It was exactly as before, but this time with a vengeance! On being passed over to my father, Thumper flew at his face with his claws, and his teeth bit him through his shirt on the chest and again on the forearm, bringing blood pumping out of the deep wound. To round off the performance, he gave Dad a final scratching with his claws, leaving marks that he claims he can still see to this day. Thumper then raced into the corner of the kitchen and glowered defiantly at us, as if daring any of us to be foolish enough to try to pick him up again. Not that we were so daft – none of us wanted to go near this psychotic new arrival into our home.

However, there was a point later in the evening when we decided that we didn't really want this rabid monster roaming around the house all night, savaging us in our beds, so someone somehow had to get Thumper back into his shiny new hutch. I was frankly terrified, so was Mum – and, if he's truthful, so was Dad! He was no coward – he was a veteran of Dunkirk and a D-Day winner of the Military Cross – but he didn't want to go anywhere near the raging rabbit.

In the end, Nanny walked across to him, said a cheery

'Come here, Thumper', and up he popped into her arms before scampering into his spacious new cage, where a feast of carrots awaited him.

And so it went on for several years. I don't know what the rest of the family had ever done to upset Thumper, but we clearly had. In or out of the house, even in his spacious new run in the garden, he would contentedly play all day; but everyone was savagely attacked on sight, including Mum, Dad, myself and (as we discovered to our embarrassment) other people's children, aunts, uncles – even the vicar. He clearly hated the very sight of us all. But, if Nanny Cox called his name, his long ears would prick up, his whiskers would bristle with pleasure and he would allow himself to be stroked all afternoon.

For the rest of us, though, there were only scratches, bites, tears and blood every single time. Trying to share a gentle moment with Thumper was like trying to take afternoon tea with Hannibal Lecter ...

4

Bunnies Behaving Badly

Freaks of nature aside, bunnies are not born bad – they become bad. There are all sorts of reasons why this might happen: bad rearing, inattentive owners, diet, handling, living conditions and many other influences can be responsible for changing the meek and mild creatures that they are into untamed monsters. Thankfully, this means that, with a bit of work, the situation can be reversed.

Domestic rabbits are not the same as wild rabbits. In the wild, evolution and natural selection are given free reign – the weak and ill die off, effectively eliminating 'defective' genes. This is not the case with the domestic rabbit. Selective breeding, plus the fact that vets can treat many of the illnesses that would be fatal in the wild, means that domestic rabbits are not only physically different to wild rabbits, but they also have hugely different temperaments. In general, domestic rabbits are friendly, sociable creatures. That said, and as we have already discovered, domestic rabbits do have certain characteristics that can be traced back to their wild ancestry. They are a long way down the food chain and are designed to survive the ravages of the wild, both mentally and physically. Placed in this high-risk-of-being-eaten category, they are therefore naturally predisposed towards fear, so it is perfectly normal for them to react to any strange sight, sound, smell or action by taking flight or acting in self-defence. Under threat, even the best-behaved bunnies will resort to their wild instincts. These instincts can be exacerbated by other factors, such as:

- the breed of rabbit – certain breeds are more docile, others tend to be more aggressive
- upbringing – if a rabbit has had a bad upbringing, the chances are that it will be worse behaved
- stress – if a rabbit feels uncomfortable, scared or otherwise out of sorts, it may exhibit unsociable tendencies

However, if a rabbit that is usually friendly turns bandit, something is wrong – and it is up to you to search for clues. Use the following checklist to ensure you haven't neglected anything:

- Is it ill or in pain?
- Is it frightened?
- Is it hungry or dehydrated?
- Is the hutch too small?
- Is there a new hutch companion?
- Is it bored?
- Is it too cold or, more likely, too hot?
- Is it neglected and lonely?

It is up to you to be on the lookout for the rabbit's needs – after all, it can't tell you itself!

Habitual bad behaviour, on the other hand, is a very different matter. It is completely out of character for domestic rabbits and is unacceptable. Often it is a case of bad upbringing – if you have a rescue animal that has been poorly treated in the past, this may well be the reason why it is being antisocial. You will need to be sympathetic and have a lot of patience if you are to overcome the problem. Here are some of the major symptoms of bad behaviour that you might observe in your rabbit, along with suggestions about how to deal with them:

AGGRESSION

If aggravated, rabbits will eventually become aggressive. They are warning you that they are on the offensive and are prepared to attack. Ignore these warning signs and they most probably will. Ovulating and pregnant does tend to get aggressive, but this is usually a passing phase. Seemingly unprovoked aggression should be investigated. It could be that the rabbit is suffering in some way, but, if the aggression genuinely seems to have no cause, it should not be tolerated.

THE REMEDY

Remove the provocation. If there are children in the household, never leave them unsupervised with the rabbit. They may not mean any harm, but they do not always understand that rabbits are living things and should not be poked and prodded or handled like toys.

If the rabbit is being frightened by other family pets, keep them away until they are properly introduced (see pages 76-81). If, even after a proper introduction, it really doesn't work out, you will have to keep them apart.

Hormonal mood swings are of course erratic, so, if you suspect that is the cause of the aggression, leave the doe to cool off for a while before you start to coax her out of it. Let her come to you and show her you care by offering her a tasty treat – a piece of apple perhaps – or by giving her a reassuring cuddle (although you should be extra gentle if you suspect she is pregnant; if she is in the later stages of pregnancy, don't lift her up at all).

Check for external sores and areas of pain. If you find no obvious reason for aggression, consult a vet: it could be an internal problem.

BITING

When a rabbit in the wild is being chased, its natural reaction is to panic and run back to its burrow or place of safety. If it gets trapped into a corner without any escape routes, it will defend itself. It is a fear-driven reaction to save its skin, and their most powerful and most debilitating form of self-defence is to bite.

No matter how well you think your pet rabbit knows and trusts you, it may misinterpret your actions if you try to catch it. You can't blame it for thinking the worst. It is not a personal attack; it is a natural reaction born from the need of rabbits to protect themselves, their territory and their babies. Be aware that punishment by shouting or smacking will only exacerbate the situation and create a vicious circle.

If your rabbit bites when you go to feed it or clean out its hutch, it is because it thinks you are invading its territory. All it is doing is protecting its food and its domain. If there are newborn babies, nursing does will fiercely guard and protect their young. Get too close and she will feel you are threatening their safety. If your rabbit is not used to people, or to being handled, the chances are that it will consider any person who approaches it to be an enemy. Establishing that you are not a threat takes time and patience.

THE REMEDY

Rabbits identify their surroundings and companions by familiar smells. If you have a biter, wear a pair of sturdy gloves when you approach and try to pick it up. A calm and soothing voice works wonders in building up confidence. As the rabbit gets gradually more used to you, remove the gloves so that it can get used to your scent. Once it feels it knows you, it will feel safe; as the fear factor subsides, so should the need for it to bite.

If biting continues, it may be that the rabbit is trying to establish its dominance. You need to make it clear to your rabbit that you are the dominant one in this relationship, but you need to do so gently. Make a noise when you are bitten, and then gently push the rabbit's head towards the floor. It won't hurt but it will teach it to respect you. If your rabbit continuously bites you when it is out of its hutch, simply put it back. It will soon come to understand that, if it bites, its freedom will be restricted, which should be an effective deterrent.

FOOD VIOLENCE

Rabbits are genetically designed to have to compete for food – they don't have a kindly owner giving them a yummy bowl of rabbit pellets once a day in the wild. For this reason, some rabbits can be aggressive at mealtimes – they see their food, they see your hand and they mistakenly assume that your hand is going to remove the food, so they take action. You should also be aware that a hand coming to a food source and then moving away is rather like, in your pet's eyes, another rabbit coming to see what is there and then retreating. Seen in this way, it is less surprising that rabbits become violent when food is involved.

THE REMEDY
Don't put the food bowl in the same place every time. If your rabbit's food is always in the same part of the hutch, it could be that it has become territorial about that area and feel that it has to defend it from intruders, i.e. you!

It might also help if you occasionally feed your rabbit by hand – that way it will come to associate your hand with the giving, rather than the taking away, of food.

GBH

Rabbits are highly territorial animals, so any form of GBH such as scratching, nipping or kicking is aimed at stopping you from getting too close. Even other rabbits are asking for trouble if they get caught trespassing.

THE REMEDY

Don't ignore the warning. Rabbits do not deliberately want to harm; they are just showing you that you are not welcome. Don't approach a doe and her newborn babies unless absolutely necessary.

Rabbits are fearful of anything strange, so, if you are a stranger, let the rabbit get used to your voice and smell. Rubbing your hands in its bedding, or holding tufts of its moulted fur, will dilute the strength of your scent. Wait for it to come to you. Rabbits are curious creatures and it will want to investigate, but don't attempt to stroke it too soon, as it might think you are about to strike.

CHEWING

In the wild, rabbits spend around four hours a day nibbling grass and chewing on hard roots and wood. Apart from satisfying their need to eat, chewing on hard materials keeps their teeth – which are constantly growing – nicely trimmed. The dried foods that domestic rabbits are given do this to some extent, but they don't adequately compensate for the tools of nature.

Domestic rabbits – particularly if bored or not getting enough hard things to chew on – will go for literally anything they can get their teeth into. If they are in the house, this can include your wooden furniture and even your wire cabling – so bang go your lights, TV and hi-fi!

THE REMEDY

To compensate, re-create! Provide bark-covered logs for your rabbit to gnaw and strip bare instead – but do make sure that the logs haven't been sprayed with any dangerous insecticides or pesticides. Hard, crunchy vegetables like carrots and apples are also good dental materials, as well as being healthy and welcome treats. A less natural alternative are gnawing blocks, but, if your rabbit gets used to these, there is no way you can reasonably expect it to tell the difference between these and your best wooden furniture. The best way to stop your rabbit from eating what it shouldn't is to say 'no' in a firm, but not frightening, voice every time it gets stuck in. You could spray the vandalised areas with chew repellents, or wrap them with protective materials, but in the long run it is less time-consuming and considerably less expensive to train your rabbit not to eat what you don't want it to.

If your rabbit is chewing things out of boredom, as is sometimes the case, you could perhaps make it work a little harder for its food. Try hanging pieces of vegetable from the roof of its hutch so it has to get up on its hind legs to reach them, or hide its food under flowerpots when it is in its rabbit run. Tricks like this will keep your rabbit's mind off destroying your furniture!

DIGGING

Rabbits are natural diggers. In the wild it is the female's job to dig the burrows and create new nests for each litter, so females tend to be the main offenders, but both sexes forage for roots to eat, particularly in winter when food on the ground is in shorter supply. The process of burrowing also helps to keep their nails filed. Pet rabbits, like their wild cousins, can be inveterate burrowers too, and will happily dig up your flowerbeds and lawns, or dig holes in your carpet when they come indoors.

THE REMEDY

You can't really stop rabbits digging – it's what they do! But you can encourage them to dig in places that suit you better. Burying food in an area where you don't mind them digging gives them a bit of a challenge and is closer to reality. Some portable rabbit runs have a wire-mesh base to stop rabbits burrowing out – and to save your lawn! You could create a mound from soil or grass instead. If your rabbit is trying to burrow through the carpet indoors, teach them to understand the word 'no'. If that proves difficult, place them in an area with a few scraps of cut-off carpet to attack, or fill a deep container with pet litter or soil.

KICKING

Rabbits don't kick up a fuss for nothing. A bruising kick buys time when they are being chased into a corner or approached from behind. If they kick when being held, it suggests that they are either in pain, are not being held correctly or simply don't want to be handled.

THE REMEDY

Don't chase your rabbit, or approach it from behind if it is in a confined space. Establish whether it has pain in its stomach, back or legs. It may not be used to being handled, or have been handled badly in the past, in which case you will need to gain your rabbit's trust before trying to handle it again. See the section on handling on pages 71-73.

LUNGEING

When we get spooked, we jump. It's the same with rabbits – when they are caught off guard, they may lunge with their front paws outstretched. If you don't back off, they may lunge a little closer. They may even make bodily contact and you will come away with a few scratches.

THE REMEDY

Don't creep up on your rabbit. Make your presence known in advance by calling its name, and always approach at a low level – as we know, prey animals are particularly fearful of anything that approaches from above. If your rabbit lunges, stay calm and introduce yourself slowly. If you don't mind a few scratches, pick it up and cuddle it – it will soon get used to your presence and realise that you are not going to harm it.

BRAWLING BUNNIES

Rabbits aren't always the gentle creatures they are made out to be. Again, this is linked to their status in the wild where, although they live in large colonies, they are forced to defend their own territory and establish their own dominance. They achieve this by brawling.

It's no surprise, therefore, that, if you have more than one animal living together, these traits should manifest themselves in domestic rabbits too. However, it is something that really must be stopped: brawling bunnies can cause each other a lot of harm – even death – if their natural instincts are left unchecked.

THE REMEDY

The spaying of females and neutering of males is to be recommended if you do not intend for them to breed. It makes them more docile and less likely to fight for sexual reasons. Two un-neutered males fight each other as a matter of course to establish dominance and may need to be kept separate from each other.

Even female rabbits will fight to establish their dominance, so, if you have two dominant male or female rabbits in the same space, you're in for trouble. Sometimes, rabbits simply have personality conflicts. In both cases, you should ideally try to keep such rabbits in separate accommodation; if you can't, then do try to feed them separately, or at least use individual bowls, as the presence of food can often be the cause of a scrap. Don't let one see you offering the other a treat; and make sure their accommodation has enough areas for them both to hide away – it is very important that rabbits should be allowed to do this, if they feel the need.

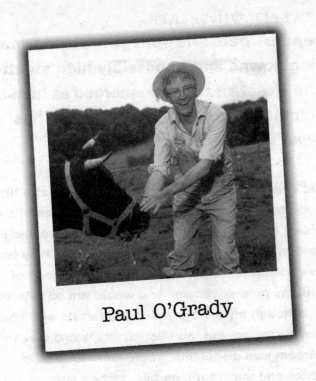

Paul O'Grady

Animal Crackers

He made his name as the infamous Lily Savage, the bee-hived, peroxide blonde bombshell with the tarty, tell-tale black roots whose wicked wit and barbed quips made Paul one of the UK's most entertaining TV personalities. Having got *Blankety Blank* and *The Lily Savage Show* under his suspender belt, he put the trade-mark evening gowns and impossibly high stilettos into the closet and has re-emerged as himself, the inimitable, equally irrepressible host of *The Paul O'Grady Show.*

As a kid I always had at least four or five pets at a time. I had rabbits, ferrets, guinea pigs, mice, rats, gerbils – everything! My brother and sister weren't interested in pets, and my parents couldn't stand them but they let me have whatever I wanted, which was very good of them. All my pets were tame and would run all over the house, although my mother hated the ferrets and when they came running into the kitchen she would scream! My bedroom was disgusting. There were rabbits in shoeboxes and mice, rats, gerbils, guinea pigs, hamsters – you name it – everywhere. And I always had animals in my pockets. Even now, I will always have an animal with me, even on tour. I used to take a budgie but now I usually take one of my dogs.

I have never been without pets, but after I left home I only had a cat or a dog. Now I've got three goats, a cow called Dot, two calves and two pigs called Blanche and Jane, named after the Hudson sisters in the film *Whatever Happened to Baby Jane?* because they are also sisters and always attacking each other. I have also got five geese and twelve goslings, but they are going – they are so evil! They're like the Gestapo. The big male is called the Führer, because that's what he's like, and the smaller ones are called Hesse and Himmler. Then there are the females, Eva Braun and Irma Grese, and their babies I call the Hitler Youth! I got them because I liked them, but, when they turn, they are vicious. They are not too bad with me, but with anyone else they are the most evil creatures alive! They are very protective and better than any guard dog or alarm. At night they parade around the house like an army. If they hear a noise, there's an unholy racket and, if they see anyone approaching, they scream.

I've also got about twenty chickens, a rooster, two dogs, a Lovebird and lots of rabbits! I hadn't thought of getting rabbits but a girl who works in my local pub was selling them. There were two I really fancied and she gave them to me for nothing. She must have been desperate to get rid of them! I called them Pod and Hobbley and then they bred and produced all these babies. All my animals have names and I called one of the babies Baby Jessica because she is so beautiful and sexy. She's a fabulous apricot colour but I haven't got a clue what breed she is – only that she has a bit of Angora in her. She recently gave birth to one that is the spit of her. The dad is small and white just like a magician's rabbit.

As for breeding more rabbits in the future, I am calling it a day. The expression 'They breed like rabbits' is so true. If you get a male and a female, be warned. Overnight they'll produce six or seven rabbits. It's endless and I'm running out of names! I'm having separate runs made so from now on the males and females will be living separately. I'm also getting the mum and dad neutered, but I was delighted when they reproduced and I really like having baby rabbits. They're no hassle to me and I can always find homes for them, but everyone else says it should be avoided. Jo Brand is having two of the babies and I have already found good homes for all the others. With proper supervision, I think rabbits are perfect pets for children because they are very easy animals to care for and will be fine as long as they are given a sensible diet and lots of space.

I feed mine on dried food and give them fresh fruit, dandelion leaves, chickweed, wild rocket and that sort of thing. They need plenty of fresh water too. A bottle on the side of the cage is perfect and the cage or living area must always be kept clean. It's as easy as that!

Short-haired rabbits don't need much grooming, and, even though Jessica has slightly longer fur, I don't need to groom her every day. But I do handle my rabbits every day because it keeps them tame. I pick them all up and, apart from one, they never struggle. Other than that, I just let them get on with it. They are lovely.

There are many reasons for promoting rabbits as pets. They are very docile and easy to look after, and a great introductory pets for kids. Kids get great pleasure from feeding them, stroking them and cleaning them out. I think rabbits are wonderful for adults as well.

A friend of mine has a big grey rabbit that runs

around the house. It's gorgeous but I wouldn't have a house rabbit unless I lived in a flat. I once had a bushbaby but it had to go to the zoo because it wrecked the place! I've got two Shih-Tzu dogs and they are fearsome. All they want to do is kill the rabbits and chickens. As soon as Buster is up and out, he's by the chicken run. He's like a Japanese guard in a prisoner of war camp. He spends his entire day pacing around, looking to find a way in. Buster has been up for various counts of murder. He's a serial chicken killer.

I've got lots of space at my house in Kent – 160 acres with woodland. It's like a fairytale when the bluebells are out. After 28 years of living in London it took me a year to get over the shock of moving to the country. I was bored and I started worrying about the Aga and all the other things that go with country living. It's a completely different way of life and at one point I thought of selling up.

Now I am settled, but I'm busy from the minute I get up. I milk the cows, change the hay, clean out the pigs and ride my horse – oh, and look after my rabbits, of course. People in the countryside work non-stop, from morning to night, and never get time to watch TV. But I love it and count my blessings. I wouldn't change it for the world.

5

Understanding Rabbits

Dr Doolittle could talk to the animals, so why shouldn't we? Well, we obviously can't have an engaging two-way conversation with them, but that does not mean we cannot learn to understand their behaviour and even communicate with them on a basic level. In order to do this, however, we need to understand how their bodies work and look at what their body language means.

BIOLOGY

THE DIGESTIVE SYSTEM

Rabbits cannot fully digest their food in one go, so their digestive system works in a somewhat unusual way to get the best out of their naturally high-fibre, low-nutrient diet. The process, known as pseudo-rumination, is carried out in two stages. The first partially breaks down the food into smaller, more manageable parcels called caecotrophs. These are passed as light, soft droppings delivered in a thin film of mucous and they contain valuable nutrients, which the rabbit cannot afford to waste.

These soft droppings, therefore, are then reingested as soon as they are excreted, then excreted again as the darker, harder, drier little pellets we know as rabbit droppings, from which all the vitamins and minerals have been extracted and absorbed into the system.

THE EARS

Comical as they may appear, a rabbit's characteristically long, pointed ears are seriously clever little instruments. In the wild, rabbits rely heavily on their ears to sound out danger, cool the body and demonstrate feelings.

Rabbits' ears prick up at the slightest sound and are cleverly adapted to swivel round independently, enabling them to pick up signals from different directions – along the lines of those old-fashioned, two-pronged indoor TV aerials. Being the shape they are, they perform like mini radar dishes, receiving stronger and clearer signals from a wider range. This is why rabbits do not react well to loud noises – they sound a lot louder to them than they do to us.

The ears are not only designed for the purposes of hearing. When rabbits overheat, they lift up their ears to catch the breeze and, by slightly narrowing them, they form little funnels for the air to circulate. This lowers or maintains body temperature, like a gentle fan.

The position of a rabbit's ears is also used to signify its state of mind to others. If they lie flat against the body, it shows they are frightened. If they are gently folded, it shows they feel secure.

However, as a result of selective breeding, rabbits' ears now come in all sorts of lengths, shapes and sizes, rendering certain breeds incapable of using them as nature intended. Lop-eared rabbits are a prime example. Too long to stand erect, too heavy to swivel round, they just hang there being utterly pointless. Nature designed rabbit ears to be functional; breeders designed them to be fashionable.

THE TAIL

The top of the rabbit's tail is always the same colour as the rest of its body, whereas the underneath is always white. However, this is only visible when rabbits run and jump because, as they do, they hold their tails as little higher. As a result, it acts as a silent signal to other animals that they are on the move.

From a distance, this flash of white is easy to spot and decipher: a slow 'flash-flash-stop' means they are hopping from one grazing spot to stop at another. More frequent 'flash-flash-flashes' then a 'stop', means that there is cause for concern but they have stopped to look around and are sussing out what the danger is is. A rapid, continuous 'flash-flash-flash-flash-flash' of white means that they are being pursued and have bolted.

THE EYES

Rabbits have eyes on the side of their head. The advantage of this is that they have peripheral vision; the disadvantage is that they cannot see what is directly in front of them. What the eyes don't see, however, the ears and the nose can sense. They send messages to the brain, which tell the rabbit to twist its head so that it can see what is in front of them.

THE FEET

Don't be fooled by their cute little toes and pretty paws – they are JCBs in disguise! They are strong enough to burrow through tough roots and excavate stones, so think what damage those claws can do to you: get in the way of an angry rabbit and you'll be scratched to ribbons.

Those little legs aren't so innocent, either. They have the strength to hop, skip, thump and jump, so rabbits are more than capable of using their power-packed hind legs to kick and their forelegs to punch. After a few rounds with a raging rabbit, their opponent will be left scratched, battered and bruised.

THE NOSE

A rabbit's nose is always twitching. The faster it twitches, the more agitated, excited, exhausted, fearful or curious your bunny is. A slow, rhythmical twitch shows that it is calm and happy. An almost still nose generally indicates it is resting but it can also mean it is ill. A totally still nose is like a totally still heartbeat – it signals your rabbit is no more.

THE TEETH

Rabbits spend their lives grazing. For this reason, their teeth are constantly growing – if they didn't, they would soon wear down to stumps. The flipside of this, of course, is that, if a domestic rabbit is not given enough hard material to chew on, its teeth will continue to grow and will get too long, leading to feeding and other related problems.

BODY LANGUAGE

Now that we have a basic understanding of the parts of a rabbit's body, we can look at some of the common forms of body language rabbits exhibit, so that you can have an idea of what it is trying to tell you.

CHINNING

Male and female rabbits have glands situated in their chin, which release a scent when activated by gentle rubbing or scratching. When a rabbit is seen rubbing its chin against objects, it is stimulating those glands and personalising those areas with traces of its smell. Although humans cannot detect it, other rabbits can and each has its own scent, enabling them to identify each other, as well as their own surroundings.

In the wild this is particularly useful when a rabbit finds itself in unfamiliar surroundings or ventures beyond its normal boundaries. It also enables the rabbit to mark out its own boundary lines as a warning to other rabbits that this is its territory. Domestic rabbits are doing exactly the same thing, and should be allowed to continue doing so. The secretion is completely harmless and undetectable to humans, but the process of spreading it will make your rabbit feel safe and secure within its own territory.

THUMPING

In the wild, rabbits really do thump their back legs just as you see them doing in cartoons. As mentioned earlier in this chapter, rabbits have very sensitive hearing and the vibrations from the thumping of their back legs can travel long distances above and below ground. These two factors combined make this a very effective warning signal to other rabbits. So, if you see your domestic rabbit thumping, it means it is trying to warn you about what it perceives to be danger nearby. Be careful approaching your rabbit when it is is doing this – it is likely to be distressed about something – so check that there really isn't anything to be concerned about nearby.

EAR MOVEMENT

The movement and positioning of the ears says more about your rabbit than practically any other body language. If they are upright and pointing as far forward as possible, it means the rabbit is inquisitive and alert. If they are apart and facing slightly forward, it means the rabbit is displaying a degree of interest in a distant object. If they are pressed flat, it could mean one of two things, depending on the context: either the rabbit is feeling angry, afraid or aggressive, or it is feeling tired or relaxed. When a rabbit starts shaking its ears, it means that it is unhappy about something: perhaps it has smelled something that makes it feel uncomfortable; perhaps it just wants to be left alone; but it can also mean that it's feeling frisky and playful. However, if a rabbit shakes its ears continuously and frequently, it may well be a sign of a medical problem and it should be referred to a vet.

TOOTH GRINDING

There are two kinds of tooth grinding that you should listen out for. One of them is sometimes referred to as purring; in fact, it is a soft chattering of the teeth that indicates the rabbit is feeling content. Rabbits can often be heard 'purring' when being stroked.

The other type of tooth grinding is very different. It is louder, for a start – though still relatively quiet to the human ear – and derives from a slower, more deliberate movement. This generally indicates that something is wrong – the rabbit may be feeling fearful, distressed or is possibly in pain. It is often accompanied by other warning signs such as bulging eyes or ears flat against the head. If it continues, you should consult a vet immediately.

BODY POSITION

It is easy to get confused between the position of squatting and the position of flattening, as they mean very different things. Squatting is a position of comfort; it shows your rabbit is feeling relaxed. However, if your pet is closer to the ground, with its ears pressed down behind its head, this is known as flattening and indicates that your rabbit is feeling fearful, especially if the muscles are tight and the eyes bulging.

Another common body position that causes confusion is when rabbits lie on their side with their legs splayed out. This does not indicate illness, rather that the rabbit is incredibly relaxed, or else is tired and needs to sleep, so, if you see your rabbit in this position, just leave it alone.

LICKING AND NOSE RUBBING

When rabbits rub noses with each other it is a sign of affection. They will also groom each other by licking, which is a further sign that they feel comfortable and trust the other animal. If your rabbit shows signs of wanting to nuzzle and lick your hand, congratulations! It means you have gained its trust and it sees you as one of the family.

GENTLE NIPPING

While frequent, aggressive biting is often the sign of something more serious being wrong (see page 96), a little gentle nip should not be taken too seriously. Rabbits need to have ways of telling you that you are doing something a bit wrong, or simply that it has had enough of whatever it is that you are doing. The context is key, and a bit of common sense will alert you to what your rabbit is trying to tell you. Occasionally, though, a gentle nip may be a sign of affection, especially if it happens when there do not seem to be any other signs of annoyance, such as flat ears or struggling.

HOW TO TALK TO YOUR RABBIT

It may sound bizarre, but rabbits do talk – not in the way that we talk, obviously, but nevertheless they have a repertoire of sounds that have recognised meanings. For instance, in the wild, whispering to each other is a sign of intimacy, much like it is with humans. But, for practical reasons, it prevents them from being heard by predators and other animals. As you get to know your rabbit you will learn all about its own individual sounds and what they mean. But before we look at those in more detail, once more we need to consider how rabbits act in the wild in order to understand what is happening when your pet makes no sound at all.

Most animals in the wild rely on picking up distant sounds and therefore have very good hearing. Rabbits, being so low down the food chain, rely even more on their senses. If they are in distress – perhaps they are injured and so their movement is restricted –

they know that, if they make a sound, it will alert predators to their presence. To them, silence is golden and no rabbit, unless it is feeling suicidal, wants to be a sitting duck. For this reason, a distressed, fearful or injured rabbit will be perfectly quiet. As domestic rabbits are not exposed to the same threats as wild rabbits, they have become more vocal. Therefore, you need to be aware of this because the most worrying sound to come from a domestic rabbit is that of complete silence. If your pet is making no noise at all, you need to work out why. If it is not instantly clear, consult your vet – there may be an internal medical problem that needs attention.

Assuming your rabbit is making noises, however, you will want to know what they mean. The following is intended as a rough guide but, to get a more accurate understanding, the context must also be taken into account: clucking, for example, is generally a gentle sound of contentment but, if your rabbit is showing other signs of distress, it may mean something quite different:

GRUNTS AND GROWLS

More often than not, these are signs of anger or warning – much like they are with a dog. Growling is generally a noise reserved for other rabbits that are considered to be a threat, so you should interpret this as an indication that the rabbit is about to fight to defend its territory. If the growling is severe, therefore, take care: it could mean that a bite or a scratch will be forthcoming. Best to leave a growling rabbit be; it is probably just feeling grumpy about something and wants its own space, although, if it also shows any other signs of aggression, it may be that it is in pain. Keep a careful eye on it, and consult your vet if need be.

OINKS

It may sound odd, but rabbits do sometimes make an oinking sound. It is a soft, non-threatening sound associated with the mating ritual. As such, it is most common in unspayed does, although it can occur even with spayed or neutered rabbits. Its meaning varies according to the context: either the rabbit is ready to mate or it isn't in the mood! Either way it is a very gentle noise and not something to worry about.

PURRING

As mentioned earlier, in the tooth grinding section what we think of as rabbits purring like cats is actually created by grinding their teeth and can mean one of two things: a soft, gentle purr is a sign of contentment, whereas a harder, shorter purr is a sign of distress, or that there may be problems with their teeth.

CLUCKING

A rabbit's clucking is similar to that of a chicken, only very much fainter. It indicates pleasure and approval.

HISSING

You will sometimes hear a rabbit hiss in the same way that a cat might. It is generally a warning to another rabbit to keep away; if it is directed towards you, it means the same thing!

SQUEAKS

Rabbits squeak if they are anxious, and a squeak can often be accompanied by other signs of anxiety, such as cowering or laying the ears flat against the head. Approach with care!

SCREAMING

Hopefully you will never hear a rabbit scream. It is a horrible, human-like sound, and rabbits only make it if they are in extreme fear of their life, or as an immediate reaction to pain.

Paul Daniels

White Magic

Paul first became interested in magic at the age of eleven, after reading a book called *How to Entertain at Parties* containing a few magic tricks, but it was years before he used magic as a means to entertain professionally. As a young man, juggling a grocery business by day with performing magic by night was wearing Paul out. But a summer season in

Newquay, followed by his TV debut on *Opportunity Knocks*, opened the door to a magical career in showbiz circles. Paul hosted numerous TV shows and *It's Magic* – the longest-running magic show ever staged in a London theatre. He is the first magician outside the USA to have been awarded the Magician of the Year by the Academy of Magical Arts. Through his books and DVDs he continues to be recognised as one of the most accomplished magicians in the world.

Magic, as we understand it, does not exist. When you go to a magic show, you are seeing an actor playing the part of a magician. It was easier to understand this when such actors were called conjurers and magicians were known as creatures of fable and legend.

Mankind is bound by certain rules of physics, whereas 'magic' apparently defies those rules. In the beginning some people started to notice, for example, that certain shaped clouds heralded the oncoming of rain. They kept this information secret so only those who knew used that knowledge to 'make rain'. Other natural phenomena were added to the store of information and those observers were the ones who became the priests of early religions, doctors of early medicine and so on. 'Magic' is therefore at the root of all science, medicine and religion.

The association of rabbits with magic goes back to 19 November 1726 when a Mary Toft was reported to have given birth to rabbits! Even the monarch's doctor was fooled by this very simple trick, but conjurers of the time knew that this so-called 'psychic' phenomenon was a trick and, by way of poking fun at the story, they started producing rabbits as part of their act. The theme was incredibly popular, and is as popular now, outlasting any pop recording!

As the top hat was the normal headgear of the day, it was very easy to borrow from a member of the audience. It was also very easy to produce handkerchiefs, bowls of water and cannonballs from a top hat, as well as being ideal for rabbits of course. Rabbits were very happy in the hat because it was just like being in a rabbit hole.

The idea of producing doves out of a silk handkerchief is artistically 'logical'. Handkerchiefs are soft and flowing, and so is the flight of the dove; they link together visually. For similar reasons, magicians' rabbits are always white because traditionally magicians dressed in black. From the back of the theatre a black rabbit would not have shown up against their costume.

I didn't own a rabbit as a child: that came a lot later! Since then I've had five, although never more than two at a time, but now I don't own any because my current show does not include tricks with rabbits. When I did use rabbits, years ago, I would buy them from a breeder. The Netherland Dwarf is the only breed to use for a magician because they do not grow large and are comfortable in the hat. A rabbit does not need special training to be a magician's helper; it just needs to be handled a lot, fed regularly and well looked after. I had one rabbit that did three years of summer seasons but then I gave it away because I wasn't going to perform the trick in the coming months, and taking it with me on the road was not my idea of taking full care of a rabbit. On the road they lived in cases that were specially made for them, like flight cases, but they were always assigned their own dressing rooms!

I think it is very cruel to pull a rabbit up by its ears and, despite the cartoon drawings, I don't know of anyone who does that in the magic world. Magicians know the dangers and want to have happy animals for as long as possible. Good care makes for a better show and they should never put the animal at any risk. Before anyone thinks about using a rabbit they should get books on rabbit care and study the articles on the Internet first. There is no 'easy' when it comes to working with animals and birds. You have to do your homework, no matter what you pick to work with. Rabbits are nice and cuddly, and they make marvellous pets; but pets must be cared for.

6

What to Do if Your Rabbit is Ill

Wild rabbits are naturally stronger than those kept as pets. Their senses are keener, their instincts sharper and the fact that they are subject to the rigours of natural selection means that the weaker specimens are more likely to die out, leaving the stronger, healthier animal to multiply. While basic day-to-day activities such as searching for food, escaping predators or simply playing in the fields keep them attuned and alert, their immune system is constantly challenged by being exposed to environmental changes and diseases.

Domestic rabbits, in that sense, are genetically different. Having been brought into the safety of the home, they have become more reliant on humans to provide what they need and protect them from harm, and they are therefore less resilient than their wild cousins. We protect them from predators, so, if a domestic rabbit dies prematurely, it is more likely to be for health reasons than the fact it became a hearty meal. Through domestication and the intervention of medicine, domestic rabbits live an average of three to eight years, depending on breed; in exceptional circumstances they can live into their teens. Most diseases and illnesses are treatable if caught early.

This chapter lists some of the more common rabbit illnesses. Before we look at these, however, it is a good idea for you to be aware of certain telltale signs that your rabbit is unwell:

- Obesity
- Weight loss
- Overgrown teeth
- A dull coat
- Scabs or inflammation on the ears
- Weeping eyes
- Bloodshot eyes
- Lumps and bumps
- A runny nose
- Sores on the skin
- Excrement on the fur around the bottom

If your rabbit exhibits any of the above symptoms, the chances are that all is not well. The following pages should give you some idea of what is the matter, but, if you are in any doubt at all, contact your vet for advice.

COMMON AILMENTS

AGORAPHOBIA

Wild rabbits hate being in wide, open spaces. They are easily spotted by predators from on high and at ground level so, although they are often seen frolicking in fields or nibbling grass verges, you will notice that they are never far from woodland or a place of safety, to which they can beat a hasty retreat when they are feeling threatened.

As a remnant of this, although domestic rabbits need large hutches to give them plenty of room to manoeuvre, less-tame rabbits may still feel threatened by ground-level approaches unless there are less-exposed areas for them to hide in. In severe cases this can lead to a form of agoraphobia, particularly if they are not used to people or do not like being handled.

Hutches should always be covered, as they fear attack from above. Hutches traditionally have a separate closed-in compartment offering a private enclosure for the rabbit to run to, as they would in the wild. Likewise, outside runs should have a sheltered area to protect the rabbit from other animals, as well as the weather. A wooden weatherproof box or smaller hutch within will suffice, as will drainpipes and pots for playing and hiding in. Think big, by all means, but remember our pet rabbits are inherently afraid of the big, bad, wild world they originally came from.

ANOREXIA

It is extremely rare for a young and healthy rabbit to stop eating deliberately. Like anorexia nervosa in humans, the condition reflects an inner state of mind commonly associated with a sudden change in personal circumstances. The loss of an owner or close lifelong companion can sometimes lead to a loss of appetite. It can also be triggered by feelings of fear or insecurity brought on by bad living conditions, neglect or cruelty. A change in diet or ownership cannot be discounted either. All these are relevant factors, but the will to stop eating is usually only temporary. Be patient and, with a lot of love, care and understanding, the depression will gradually lift and your rabbit's appetite will return.

If emotional factors do not seem to be relevant, it may be that a physical condition is stopping the rabbit from eating. A dislocated jaw, for example, may hamper a rabbit's ability to eat. If you suspect there is a problem, you must consult your vet.

When an old rabbit stops eating, the sad truth is that it is probably nearing the end of its life. Most vets will suggest that it would be kinder to put it to sleep.

BORDETELLOSIS

This is a bacterial infection that causes a bronchial disease. The symptoms are heavy breathing, sneezing, matted fur from wiping a runny nose, listlessness and lack of appetite. If you suspect bordetellosis, you should consult your vet immediately: not only is it very uncomfortable for the rabbit, but it can also lead to more complicated diseases such as pneumonia (see page 142). Your vet may need to take an X-ray to make a full diagnosis.

CONSTIPATION

It is highly unusual for rabbits to suffer from constipation. Their fibre-rich diet automatically keeps them regular. If it does occur, though, it can be a cause for concern. As we know, rabbit droppings do not go to waste because they are reingested so that the full complement of nutrients are extracted from the rabbit's food. In the wild, droppings have additional functions too: they are used to mark boundaries and are left as a trail, should the rabbit stray further afield. So a bunged-up bunny is not only uncomfortable; it means the rabbit is unable to benefit from the other functions of its droppings.

Infrequent, irregular bowel movements or small, hard, dry pellets probably mean that your rabbit is not getting enough fresh greens, or that it is dehydrated. Do not ignore these symptoms – left unresolved, it will lead to more serious problems and make your rabbit very ill. You need to up the fibre content of your rabbit's diet. Lots of fresh greens will help straight away, and make sure that your rabbit has plenty of fresh, clean water. Never let the bottle run dry, and make sure the water is changed every day, especially in the summer when it has a tendency to go green. If the condition persists for more than a couple of days, or if there are no droppings whatsoever, call a vet: there could be a blockage and that is serious.

DIARRHOEA

Again, wild rabbits very rarely get diarrhoea: they know which plants are poisonous and which to eat, and they eat according to the body's needs. But pet rabbits are not always given the same choices. The most common cause of diarrhoea is too many greens and not enough starch in the diet. Rabbits often suffer from the condition when they are put in a run at the beginning of spring, when new grass is shooting, or if they have access to certain astringent plants such as Shepherd's Purse or raspberry and blackberry leaves. Withdrawing these from the diet for a couple of days, or moving the run to a stony area where access to grass is restricted, should get your rabbit back to normal; if not, there could be internal problems which should be referred to a vet.

EAR CANKER/EAR MITES

Scratching one or both ears to get rid of the odd tickle is perfectly normal, but constant scratching is not. When a rabbit's ears are inflamed, scabby and sore, or it keeps shaking its head, the likelihood is that it has ear mites.

Mites are transferred through droppings, bedding or from animal to animal, so prevention is the best cure: avoid contact with infected animals and droppings, burn any infected bedding and disinfect any infected areas. Mites can be treated at home by rubbing warm oil or Vaseline over the infected areas, or you may prefer to take your rabbit to a vet.

ENTERITIS

The rabbit's digestive tract is populated by a diverse population of bacteria and other organisms, which maintain a sensitive balance, helping the rabbit to digest the food it eats. Any change to this balance can result in disorders that affect the rabbit's digestive ability and can therefore be very serious.

Enteritis is caused by the inflammation or infection of the intestines. It has a number of symptoms: diarrhoea, bloatedness, intense teeth-grinding, bulging eyes, lack of appetite and weight loss. It is generally caused by incorrect diet – particularly one that does not have enough fibre – but it can also be caused by stress, certain antibiotics and, in some cases, bacteria.

The best way to avoid enteritis is to feed your rabbit a proper, healthy diet (see pages 56-59). It is important to avoid sudden changes in your rabbit's diet too, as this can upset the balance of bacteria in the gut and lead to enteritis. If you suspect that your rabbit is suffering from the condition, consult your vet.

ENTEROTOXEMIA

This is the most serious disorder of the digestive tract. It is caused by a proliferation of harmful bacteria such as clostridium or E. coli, which produce poisonous toxins. It is most common in recently weaned rabbits, but it can be seen in any rabbit that is already showing signs of enteritis (see previous page). Symptoms of enterotoxemia can include very bad diarrhoea with traces of blood, listlessness, lack of appetite and, unfortunately, sudden death. Any suspicion that your rabbit is suffering the condition should be immediately referred to your vet.

FLEAS

Fur is a perfect breeding ground for fleas, mites and lice. The most common cause of these infestations is being in contact with other infected animals, but they can be easily treated using flea powders that can be bought over the counter or prescribed by a vet.

FLYSTRIKE

Flies are attracted to raw flesh, excrement or anything that is wet, warm and smelly where they can lay their eggs. Once hatched, the maggots will feed off decaying meat or the fresh flesh of any living animal. Flystrike is an extremely unpleasant condition whereby flies are attracted to any excrement that may be clinging to the rabbit's fur. They lay their eggs here, and, when the maggots hatch, they start to feed on the rabbit's flesh. It is a potentially common problem, particularly with breeds that have longer fur and those not kept in clean conditions. It strikes overnight and, if not treated immediately, can be fatal.

Do keep a careful eye out for sticky droppings in the hutch, or excrement stuck to the rabbit's fur that is infested with eggs or little white maggots (larvae). Left unnoticed, the maggots will worm their way under the surface of your rabbit's skin and eat their way up the rectum, leaving fragments of dead, grey flesh in their wake. If the hutch is dirty, or the area around the anus is not kept clean, it is a magnet for flies to lay their eggs. Once laid, the maggots will immediately start to feed on the skin and within twenty-four hours rabbits are truly infested. It only takes one fly to produce a large quantity of eggs and only a couple of days for the maggots to have done irreparable internal damage to their host.

If caught very early, there is a good chance your vet will be able to get rid of all the maggots. It might involve minor surgery under local anaesthetic if they have started burrowing under the skin. But, if flystrike is caught too late, there is no hope. The best cure is prevention. Never let the hutch get dirty, particularly in summer when flystrike usually occurs. Don't overcrowd the hutch and keep it well ventilated. Check your rabbit daily for the slightest hint of soiling or matting around the bottom and, in between cleaning out the hutch, remove any droppings. Ensure that their conditions are dry and that the area around the rabbit's anus is kept clean, by brushing and washing as often as is necessary.

If you do have a bout of flystrike, burn all the bedding and faeces to ensure that all the eggs and maggots are destroyed. Scrub the hutch clean using a mild detergent such as washing-up liquid and disinfect. Always make sure the hutch is completely dry before reusing.

HAIR BALLS

Each time a rabbit licks itself clean – which is several times a day – small amounts of hair are ingested. This is not normally a problem as they are expelled as part of the normal digestive process. However, if there is not enough fibre or water in the diet, these fine hairs will accumulate and eventually form hair balls, which can cause a blockage in the digestive tract and lead to serious problems – yet another reason to ensure your rabbit is eating properly! Long-haired breeds are naturally more prone to hair balls, so it is essential to keep them well brushed and groomed – particularly when they are moulting – to prevent them swallowing excessive hairs.

HEAD TILT

If your rabbit's head appears lopsided and your pet loses its balance, it could be suffering from a condition known as head tilt. The most likely cause of this is an ear infection. However, if there are no signs of scabs or mites (see page 139), it is possible that your rabbit has a parasite infecting the brain, or has suffered a mild stroke, so you should consult your vet.

HEATSTROKE

As previously mentioned, rabbits are very sensitive to heat. Heatstroke can be caused by the animal being kept in a badly ventilated area or by being exposed to excessive heat, either by being positioned next to a hot fire or radiator, or in direct sunlight. The major symptoms of heatstroke are panting, floppiness and severe lack of energy. Your rabbit may also flop on to one side.

Never be tempted to plunge a rabbit into cold water: this can cause a severe, even fatal, shock. Instead, encourage them to drink plenty of water – but it should never be straight from the fridge or too cold, as that can also cause shock. You can bring the body temperature down by gently spraying their ears with cool water, placing a towel dampened with cool water across its shoulders, or wrapping its body in a cool, damp towel. Immediately relocate the housing and run to a shaded and well-ventilated area away from direct sunlight or sources of excessive heat.

LICE

Rabbits can have lice in the same way that humans can. The symptoms are furious bouts of scratching, and you may find little white eggs attached to the fur when you are grooming your pet.

Lice can be fairly easily eliminated using special powders available over the counter or from your vet.

LUMPS AND BUMPS

The good news is that most lumps and bumps are rarely cancerous – they are usually no more than an abscess caused by an external wound that has become infected, or cysts. In short-haired breeds, such lumps are easier to spot – the fur appears to be 'flowering' – but, other than by stroking, slight swellings often go undetected.

Rabbits have sensitive skin, so wounds can be caused by simple objects: rusty nails or screws that have worked their way loose in the hutch or run could turn superficial wounds septic; coarse bedding straw or brittle hay can pierce the skin. It's also not uncommon for cheap hay to contain harmful objects or wire.

Wounds should be treated with antiseptic ointment, or your vet may prescribe antibiotics if they are caused by bacterial infection.

MALOCCLUSION

Unfortunately, hereditary malocclusion is a fairly common problem with rabbits. It occurs when the teeth are incorrectly aligned. As mentioned earlier, rabbits' teeth are constantly growing. If they are not correctly aligned, they will not wear down properly. The result is that the teeth grow too long and prevent rabbits from chewing and eating properly.

When rabbits in the wild suffer from malocclusion, they starve to death. For this reason, some vets may recommend that a newborn rabbit with malocclusion is put down, in order to prevent the condition from being passed from one generation to another and, in old rabbits, to prevent suffering. My rabbit Warren(etta) was born with hereditary malocclusion and, because she was so ill, my vet gave me three options: to have her put down, to have her teeth extracted, or to have her teeth filed down every few weeks.

I discounted the first option immediately. To have her put down would have been impossible for me. The second option was drastic: removing her teeth needed to be done under anaesthetic and, considering she was already weak, there was a greater risk she may not have survived. It also meant that her diet would have to change dramatically from hard food to soft food. Carrots and other hard fruit and vegetables would have to be shredded, as well as reducing bigger pieces to more manageable portions. The third option was the least invasive, but I felt it would be terrifying for Warren(etta) to have her teeth filed down every six weeks.

Moreover, for many people this option is simply impossible to fit around their other commitments.

After careful consideration, I chose to have Warren(etta)'s teeth extracted and, on balance, I think I chose the best option. I felt that, as she got older, she would be less and less able to deal with the trauma of having her teeth filed, and would eventually have had to have her teeth removed under anaesthetic after all.

MANGE

Mange is a skin disease caused by mites, which are often to be found on rabbits' ears. However, they can also affect the rest of the body. Symptoms of mange infestation include constant scratching, patchy hair loss, scaly skin and dull fur. If you suspect mange mites, check the skin for little black particles and treat it with proprietary insect powders, which can be bought over the counter or from your vet. If you have a rabbit infected with mange, it is important to ensure that it does not come into contact with other rabbits and companion pets, and to thoroughly disinfect the rabbit's hutch and run.

MASTITIS

Lactating does can suffer from inflamed teats in the same way that some women do when breastfeeding. If your lactating doe has cracked and sore teats, it is likely to be suffering from mastitis and should be seen immediately by a vet. If the condition is serious it can be fatal in rabbits, but is treatable with antibiotics. Be aware, however, that rabbits that are undergoing a course of antibiotics should not be allowed to breastfeed, as antibiotics can be dangerous for kittens. In less severe cases, you can soothe the symptoms by placing a warm towel over the affected area.

MITES

Rabbits often get mites. It happens particularly if there are other pets around, or if the bedding is infected. Flea powders will get rid of them but, as a precaution, regularly disinfect the areas your rabbit inhabits and burn old bedding to stop them spreading. The early signs are small bald patches, so look out for mites burrowing under the skin before the condition worsens.

MYXOMATOSIS

Myxomatosis, along with VHD, is one of the two diseases against which your rabbit really must be vaccinated at an early age. It was introduced to wild rabbits deliberately as a means of keeping down the population – something it did very effectively. Myxomatosis is spread by mosquitoes and other flying insects, and its symptoms include fever, discharge from the eyes, listlessness and swelling of the genitals and face. If your rabbit has not been vaccinated, and you suspect myxomatosis, consult your vet immediately. If caught early enough, it can be cured; left too late, it is fatal.

MUCOID ENTERITIS

The causes of mucoid enteritis are something of a medical mystery. Symptoms include diarrhoea, lack of appetite, extreme weight loss, listlessness and feverishness. It is most common in five- to eight-week-old rabbits, and also does during late pregnancy and early in their lactation period.

Several years' research has detected a vague pattern that suggests that any radical change in diet may be to blame. It can also follow a sudden increase in weather temperatures, and it is seen more regularly in certain breeds – which indicates that it could even be hereditary.

As the cause is uncertain, there is no defined cure but, as it is linked to a change in diet and climate, as a precaution, make sure your rabbit is kept in a reasonably even temperature and new foods are introduced gradually. Antibiotics sometimes work, but prevention is very much the best cure.

OBESITY

Obesity is not technically a disease because it cannot be caught, but, once it starts, it will spread and get out of control. If this happens, it is time to take stock. You will never see a fat rabbit in the wild: they eat what they need to sustain a healthy lifestyle and levels of energy, and are kept trim by their natural urge to play, run and search for food. It is normal for both wild and tamed rabbits to develop a thicker coat and carry a thin layer of extra fat for added warmth, but an overly fat domestic bunny will soon become an unhealthy one, so monitor what it eats and regulate its diet!

If your rabbit is on a well-balanced diet, as it should be, it could be that it is having too many treats added to its diet. Cut down on unhealthy treats and replace them with carrots, apples and other hard fruits or vegetables. Pellets contain the right proportions of fats, proteins, carbohydrates, vitamins and minerals, so changing from mixed feeds to pellets gives your rabbit no choice but to eat what it is given.

If you are convinced that the diet is OK, the chances are that your rabbit is not getting enough exercise. If confined to a hutch, make sure it is large enough for the rabbit to stretch, hop and move around freely. In summer or mild, dry, wintry climates, let your rabbit loose in a run, or create a secure area indoors where it can unleash its energy and loosen its joints. For more information on suitable accommodation for rabbits, see page 49.

PARALYSIS

Rabbits have a real fear of heights, and can sustain terrible injuries if they have a fall. If your rabbit has a fall from a height, or is dropped, and seems to stop moving, it may well have sustained a serious back or neck injury and will need urgent attention. Try not to move it until you have consulted your vet.

Rabbits can also undergo temporary paralysis if they experience some sort of trauma – the 'rabbit-in-headlights' syndrome. This 'freezing' is usually only temporary: if possible, return the rabbit to its normal environment, where it will feel safe and should soon recover, but do make sure you handle it gently and don't exert any pressure on its back. If in doubt, seek medical advice.

PARASITES OF THE INTESTINE

These parasites include tapeworms and pinworms. The symptoms of infection by such parasites include a distended abdomen, worms around the bottom, a dull coat and weight loss (even though your rabbit appears to be eating heartily). Sometimes there are no outward symptoms and your vet will have to examine some of your rabbit's droppings in order to tell if intestinal parasites are present. They can be treated either by a medicine, which is administered orally, or by injection.

Rabbits kept in unhygienic conditions are prone to getting worms, but you can make your pet less susceptible to them by ensuring it avoids areas where cats and dogs have fouled.

PNEUMONIA

Pneumonia in rabbits, as in humans, is a very serious condition. Signs to look for include a runny nose, breathing difficulties, loss of appetite, lower body temperature and dull eyes and coat. If you suspect it, you must consult your vet immediately.

RINGWORM

This skin disease is not commonly associated with rabbits, but it can affect them quite badly. Symptoms include reddish circular sores or greyish scabs, which form rings on the surface of the skin. The condition is no different to ringworm in humans, but it looks worse because the fur falls out in affected areas, leaving little bald patches.

Ringworm is a fungal disease contracted by humans and domestic pets. It is usually carried by rodents, so make sure rats and mice cannot get into the hutch or run. Ringworm can be treated by powders and medicines – your vet will advise – but it is very important that you fully disinfect the rabbit's environment after a bout of the infection.

SNUFFLES AND SNEEZES

Rabbits can catch a cold just like we can. The odd sneeze is probably just down to dust particles in the air causing nasal irritation, but constant sneezing, a runny nose, sore eyes and wet paws from wiping discharge from the rabbit's eyes and nose are all signs of a more serious cold.

At the first sign of a cold, clean and disinfect the rabbit's hutch and, if possible their popular areas around the house. Keep bunny warm and away from the cold and draughts – but remember not to let them overheat as this can cause heatstroke (see page 135). It is best to seek the advice of your vet – left untreated, it can lead to pneumonia (see page 142).

SORE HOCKS

Sitting and standing on damp, dirty flooring or thumping repeatedly on hard flooring or wire meshing can cause sore, cracked paws – also known as pododermatitis – which is very uncomfortable for your rabbit. Make sure that the bedding and flooring is always kept clean and dry. Although it is a practical measure to secure runs with wire-mesh flooring to stop your rabbit burrowing out, it is preferable that it should be buried beneath the surface.

If your rabbit does suffer from sore hocks, at the first sign apply Vaseline to the affected areas, as it will act as a barrier and prevent the cracks from becoming dirty and infected. Your vet can then treat them with a special cleanser or with antibiotics.

STICKY BOTTOM

As we know, rabbits have two types of droppings: the soft, sticky type that owners seldom see unless there is a problem; and the reingested version of these, which are expelled as the harder rabbit droppings we have come to recognise! If the softer droppings become stuck around the rabbit's fur, it can be the sign of a more serious issue.

There are a number of reasons why your rabbit may suffer from what is commonly termed 'sticky bottom'. The first is that it may be simply too fat for its mouth to reach its bottom, in which case you need to read the section on obesity (page 140). Another and possibility is that its diet is incorrect or imbalanced – and it is producing too many of these first droppings and simply can't eat them all. You need to examine its diet and make sure it is getting enough fibre. If the rabbit has mouth ulcers or the teeth are overgrown, it will be unwilling or unable to eat its droppings, so, if you suspect that might be the case, it is essential you consult your vet.

It is also absolutely vital that you do not allow sticky bottom to continue: it creates a perfect environment for infections to breed, and will make it much more likely that your rabbit will suffer the dreaded flystrike (see page 133).

SYPHILIS

As with humans, syphilis in rabbits is a sexually transmitted disease. So, if you have not had your pet neutered or spayed, you should regularly examine the genitals and face. If you encounter scabby sores, it may indicate syphilis, in which case your vet will probably recommend a course of antibiotics, which should clear it up fairly quickly.

TYZZER'S DISEASE

Tyzzer's Disease is another disorder of the digestive tract. Its symptoms are listlessness and large quantities of very watery diarrhoea. It is an extreme form of enteritis (see page 132) and is often caused for the same reason – incorrect diet. It can be fatal in old rabbits or those that have been recently weaned. If you suspect Tyzzer's Disease, consult a vet immediately. The condition is usually treated by reverting to a high-fibre, low-carbohydrate diet.

URINE BURN

This occurs when urine-soaked fur makes the skin underneath damp. It can lead to infection that will need to be cured by antibiotics, but you will have to establish the cause to stop it recurring. The most usual cause is lack of regular cleaning but, if the rabbit is young and agile, the condition may well be related to a kidney problem or infection. Older rabbits suffering from arthritis and stiffened joints are more prone to the condition as they find it difficult to position themselves, or are unable to empty properly so end up wetting their fur. If this is the case, check regularly for signs of staining around the anus and wash gently.

VIRAL HAEMORRHAGIC DISEASE (VHD)

This is a very unpleasant illness against which every rabbit really must be vaccinated in the first few weeks of its life (see page 60) as it is fatal. Symptoms include high fever, listlessness, lack of appetite, spasms and bleeding from the mouth and bottom.

WEIGHT LOSS

There are several reasons for weight loss in a healthy rabbit, and all denote an underlying condition that needs immediate, sometimes invasive action. Assuming your rabbit is not being underfed, the three main causes of weight loss are parasites (see page 141), dental problems and poisoning.

WORMS

See *Parasites of the Intestine*.

GIVING YOUR RABBIT MEDICINE

If you take your rabbit to the vet, they may well prescribe some sort of medicine. This may come in a number of forms – tablets, liquid medicines or ear drops and eye drops which are the most common – either way the chances are that your rabbit won't much like having them administered. Your vet will probably give you some guidelines on how to go about this, but it is good for you to know what is involved:

HOLDING YOUR RABBIT

It is important that you hold your rabbit firmly but gently when administering medicine, as it is likely to wriggle and try to escape if it finds it unpleasant. I find it easiest to wrap the rabbit in a warm blanket – it will find it more comforting than being handled by your bare hands, and also prevents you from being scratched – and I hold it firmly against my body to make sure it is secure. Always talk in a soothing voice while administering the medicine – it will make your rabbit feel less nervous.

TABLETS

Some rabbits will eat tablets without any problems at all; others will need to have them crushed up and added to their food, if they are to be persuaded to swallow them. If neither of these works, your vet should be able to supply you with a short stick so you can place the tablet on the end of it. This will enable you to put the tablet at the back of the rabbit's mouth, making it much easier to swallow. Personally I wouldn't recommend this unless you really know what you are doing, as it can cause damage to the throat, gums and teeth.

LIQUID MEDICINE

The best way to administer liquid medicine is to use a syringe. Hold the rabbit as described above, place the syringe in its mouth and slowly squeeze it. It *is* important to do this slowly, as rabbits cannot drink particularly quickly. Don't be tempted to place the rabbit on its back, either, as there is a chance that the medicine will be inhaled into the lungs, which may cause suffocation.

EAR DROPS

Warm up the ear drops slightly before you start. Hold your rabbit as described above, and place a drop in the ear. Then slowly massage the bottom of the ear to allow the medicine to enter the ear canal. It's not very pleasant for rabbits, so don't be surprised if it wriggles when you do this.

EYE DROPS

Hold the rabbit as described above. Gently pull down the bottom of the eyelid and – being very careful not to touch the eye with the applicator (your bunny will *not* appreciate this!) – place a drop in the well at the bottom of the eye. Let go of the eyelid and allow the rabbit to blink – this will spread the medicine around the surface of the eye.

Andrew Castle

A Cautionary Tale

Before gaining recognition as one of the breakfast-show team on GMTV, Andrew was a professional tennis player gaining the distinction of being Britain's number-one tennis champion for seven years. After retiring from professional tennis he became a member of the British Olympic Team represented in Seoul (1998) and Barcelona (1992) and is a respected sports broadcaster and commentator specialising in covering Wimbledon and other major tennis events for TV. A good sport on and off the courts, he is a very modest king of the Castle family.

We had two lop-eared rabbits, one called Bugsy and one called Snowy, but unfortunately we don't have them any more. The kids didn't want to give them as much care as they needed and, to be perfectly honest, they just got too much for me to handle. They weren't castrated either and were just beginning to get a bit aggressive, but, just before we took them to be done, someone very kindly offered to take them off our hands.

The kids wanted them. Georgina was nine and Claudia was seven, and they were at the stage that every child goes through when they think every animal is cute – and rabbits, when they are young, are very cute. They're so small and timid, and need all the love they can get. At that age, children have so much love to give and just want to give animals all the love they need. My daughters both fell into that same trap.

Had we, as parents, done any research and looked into it properly, we would have realised what we were taking on. I never had a rabbit as a kid. We just had cats and dogs, but I didn't want them again because I knew the level of commitment involved. Getting a rabbit was a compromise, yet we went into the pet shop with our eyes closed. I knew there were baby rabbits in there and I knew the people who worked there, who were all very nice, so I can't say we bought on impulse – just ignorance. We bought two rabbits, two bowls, a packet of food and a little book called *How to Look After Your Rabbit* that had lots of pictures. What was funny about the book was that it was written in rabbit language. 'My claws will need clipping if I don't get to run around properly. I don't like this to eat but I do like to eat that!' It was written for children with adults in mind and was actually very good.

It was only when our rabbits grew that we realised our mistake. They didn't get huge, but for some reason they just stopped being cute. They had lost their appeal and, because our girls hadn't grown close to them, they had lost interest.

When we bought the rabbits we thought we could tame them and have them as household pets but, when they came into the house, they chewed all the wiring including the wires to a new stereo system I had bought. I had to pay £100 just to replace that, and then had to rabbit-proof all the other wires in the house. The whole thing got so out of control and expensive that we forgot that idea and put them in the garden. To add insult to injury, they chewed through the irrigation system. It was wonderful for them, but they lacerated it. Then they attacked the lighting wires. When you turn on the lights and nothing happens, there's that sudden realisation that it's not because of the bulb but the bunny! That all had to be replaced too, so we had to keep the rabbits in a hutch and a large run, but we lived in constant fear of the foxes getting them. If Bugsy or Snowy had been killed, it would have been dreadful. It would have been a terrible injustice – but so too was keeping them in those conditions.

I felt I had to take on the responsibility of looking after them. My wife Sophia was busy enough with looking after the house and children without having to clean out their hutches and feed them, so it was only fair. But every time I fed them, I felt guilty. I knew they weren't getting enough attention or exercise, and whenever I heard them running round their hutches at night I felt worse. I tried to plot out where they could run in the garden, but they still wouldn't have had the life they deserved.

I wasn't happy about giving them away. The girls didn't want them to be separated so I had to make sure they stayed together. It wasn't easy finding them a home, though. I made lots of phone calls, then searched the internet for sanctuaries and rescue centres, but they were all full. It made me realise just how many rabbits need homes. In the end the people from our local post office heard we were trying to place them and they came to us. It was quite a trauma when they left, but at the same time it was a relief.

Georgina and Claudia now have two hamsters, which

is much more sensible as they can care for them properly. And the rabbits are in a very good new home, where they are loved and have a wonderful life. That's how it should be. They live down the road from us so the girls can visit them whenever they want, and we are always hearing about them.

I grew up with animals so I have an affinity with them. My only regret is that I couldn't provide the best life for our rabbits; but on the positive side they didn't suffer and my children learned about caring for living creatures. If you live with animals, you learn to respect them and understand their needs. The advice I would give to parents is to make sure that they know what they are getting into before buying a rabbit. They are a bit of a one-way street; but, for an older person on their own or a family that could give them lots of love and attention, they make wonderful pets.

7

Breeding

Rabbits are proverbially enthusiastic breeders! Some species can produce an overwhelming number of offspring, and it is well known that it took only 50 years for rabbits to colonise the entire continent of Australia. If you keep an un-neutered buck and an unspayed doe in the same enclosure, therefore, they will do what rabbits do, and before long they will have produced a large litter of little bunnies.

It might sound sweet, but, just because you *can* breed rabbits, it doesn't necessarily mean that you *should*. Breeding is only something you should think about once you have carefully considered all the implications – many of which I hope to cover in this chapter – and are certain it is something you want to take on. There are far too many rescue rabbits in the world, mostly as a result of thoughtless breeding.

Before we discuss breeding any further, though, I want to explain the exact opposite process.

CASTRATING AND SPAYING

Castrating a male rabbit involves removing the testicles completely; spaying a female involves removing both ovaries and the uterus. The idea of castrating or spaying a rabbit is a relatively new one and many people still feel uncomfortable with it, for a number of reasons. Historically, rabbits were rarely operated on, as the chances of them recovering from the anaesthetic were so small. Medical science has moved on a lot since those days, however, and rabbits can now be safely put under anaesthetic in order to be operated on. Other owners simply don't think of it: either they only have one rabbit, or they have a male and a female, which they keep in separate cages. Avoiding pregnancy, however, is not the only reason for neutering your rabbit. There are a good many other advantages as well, and I would urge you to consider it if you do not intend to breed.

PREVENTING PREGNANCY

Domestic rabbits should not be allowed to breed indiscriminately. If you are not set up to look after the new arrivals properly, or can't find suitable homes for them, they are likely to lead miserable lives and that is cruel.

PREVENTING FALSE PREGNANCY

False pregnancies have become a proverbial figure of fun, but in fact they can be very distressing for rabbits. False pregnancies occur when the ovaries send out a false signal, telling her she is pregnant when she is not. As a result she will start displaying some of the characteristics of pregnant rabbits. These include:

- Nesting
- Milk production (which can be very painful if there are no kittens around to relieve it and can lead to dangerous mastitis)
- An aggressive sense of territory
- They may suffer a lack of appetite, which can lead to malnutrition and other serious disorders of the digestive system.

PREVENTING CANCER OF THE UTERUS

Unspayed females, particularly those that have never been pregnant, run a much higher risk of cancer of the uterus, a disease that is incredibly common in female rabbits. Sterilisation eliminates the risk of this very malignant disease, and others such as endometritis, pyometra and uterine aneurism.

PREVENTING TESTICULAR CANCER

The medical reasons for neutering males are less compelling than the behavioural ones. However, although testicular cancer is less common in males than uterine cancer is in females, the disease is nonetheless very virulent in bucks and is usually eliminated by neutering.

PREVENTING AGGRESSIVE BEHAVIOUR

When both male and female rabbits go through the stages between puberty and sexual maturity, their personality changes. It is natural that this should be so: their bodies are responding to the need to protect themselves and their families. But this can be hugely problematic for the domestic rabbit, especially if it is living in close proximity to other rabbits. They can harm each other quite significantly, even fatally, if this aggressive behaviour is allowed to continue. This behaviour is also antisocial for humans, who have to endure unfriendly and sometimes – for small children at least – frightening behaviour from their rabbit. Sexually mature bucks also tend to spray urine around their habitat in order to mark out their territory, and some people may find this habit unpleasant and unhygienic. Neutering tends to stop them doing this.

The best age to neuter rabbits is just after they reach sexual maturity. This is generally at about the age of four to six months, although certain larger breeds do not mature until the age of nine months. There are a number of reasons for waiting. Firstly the sexual organs are not fully developed until this time, so the process is far more difficult. Secondly the physical effects of neutering a rabbit prematurely are not fully understood.

Your vet will advise you to keep an eye on your rabbit, to check that there is no unusual swelling or infection. Rabbits often suffer a slight loss of appetite following any operation, but this should disappear after a day or so, and within a few days they will have fully recovered from the procedure.

WHAT YOU SHOULD CONSIDER BEFORE YOU START BREEDING

ARE YOU BREEDING GOOD SPECIMENS?

Sadly, the world is overpopulated with too many unwanted rabbits, so please don't breed indiscriminately. A responsible breeder should make sure that their rabbits are good examples of their breeds, and that they are in good health. At the very least you should satisfy yourself that the rabbit does not suffer any inherited conditions such as malocclusion (see page 137).

ARE YOU PREPARED FOR THE COMPLICATIONS THAT MIGHT BE INVOLVED?

These include:

- the mother being unable to breastfeed, in which case all the babies will have to be bottle-fed
- the mother rejecting the babies, in which case their welfare will be entirely down to you
- some of the babies may die – you need to be prepared for this eventuality

DO YOU HAVE THE PATIENCE – AND THE MONEY – TO BREED RABBITS?

Rabbit breeding is not necessarily lucrative. Caring for litters is expensive and will probably cost a lot more than you could ever hope to make from it. Breeding also requires a lot of time and patience from you.

DO YOU HAVE GOOD HOMES IN MIND FOR YOUR LITTERS?

If you are planning to find homes for your rabbits, make sure there is a demand for them before even entertaining the idea of breeding.

HOW TO GO ABOUT BREEDING

As you might expect, rabbits need little encouragement to start breeding. Does are fertile from four months old. In the wild they will start mating as soon as they become sexually mature, but in captivity it is best to wait until they are around five or six months old, or six to seven months old for the larger breeds. Don't leave it too long to start breeding as they may have difficulty conceiving, or they may lose interest in the whole process altogether. You should stop breeding them when they reach three or four years of age. Domestic rabbits have a longer lifespan than wild rabbits, but breeding them beyond these years reduces the likelihood of them producing healthy offspring. In addition, although females *can* breed when they are past their prime, it can seriously affect their health and their lifespan if you allow them to do so. The best time to start breeding females, therefore, is between six and twelve months. Bucks reach puberty at around four to five months, and attain sexual maturity around seven months.

Rabbits are promiscuous and polygamous, so it is common to see mating between different does and bucks; it is also common to see members of the same family mating, if they are kept in the same environment. Does are fertile all year round – they don't have a menstrual cycle as such, but release eggs as a result of breeding – so in theory they could produce an average of twelve litters a year. However, the practice of intense breeding can be seriously detrimental to the health of the doe, and is very irresponsible of the owner. Indeed, in the wild, rabbits only tend to breed when food is plentiful – which generally means springtime. A maximum of three litters a year is considered safe.

Before breeding, make sure the doe has everything she needs to conceive and to feel comfortable and safe during pregnancy. In practice, this means a hutch with plenty of room, clean bedding and plenty of light – rabbits need light to stimulate ovulation. It is unwise, however, to bring the buck to the doe's hutch: if you do, there is a good chance that the doe will become protective of her territory, and if this happens she will resist the male's advances and the probability of them mating is pretty remote. Take the doe to the buck – she won't welcome the intrusion – and keep an eye on them as you do so. If they demonstrate any aggressive behaviour towards each other, separate them. This is not uncommon – it just means there is a personality clash, or the doe is disinterested. If this is the case, it is not likely that they will mate successfully. If, however, you see the buck mate the doe, you are in business. Allow them to mate a couple of times to be sure, then separate them and wait and see!

HOW TO TELL IF YOUR DOE IS PREGNANT

The gestation period for baby rabbits is about a month, but you will probably not notice any swelling of the abdomen until a good 20 days into the pregnancy. If, after this time, you don't see any swelling, take your doe to the vet: they will be able to tell by feeling the abdomen and checking for heartbeats whether any babies are present.

Swelling of the abdomen is not the only way to tell if your doe is pregnant, however. You will probably find that she starts preparing a nest for her babies. You should provide a nesting box in the sleeping area of the hutch and fill it with plenty of fresh, clean bedding. You will find that she will line her nest with fur plucked from her coat; if she does not do this, you can place some sheep's wool in the nesting box or try and salvage any rabbit fur saved from grooming in anticipation of her becoming a nursing doe.

During pregnancy, diet is of paramount importance, so make extra certain that your doe is being fed a nutritious, balanced diet, with plenty of fresh greens, hay and fresh water. Pregnant does will need more food than they required before pregnancy. Consequently, you should increase what you give them gradually over the month, so that by the end of their pregnancy they are eating about twice the amount they consumed before. Now, more than ever, you need to avoid giving them fatty foods or starchy foods such as sweet treats – these can lead to complications during the birthing process. You may find, however, that, a few days before giving birth, the doe exhibits a slight loss of appetite. This is perfectly normal and nothing to worry about. It is also important that your pregnant rabbit is given the opportunity to exercise – she needs a few hours a day (at least two – more if you can allow it) of roaming in a rabbit run to keep her health and strength up.

It is also possible that does will start to act somewhat aggressively towards you during pregnancy. Again, this is normal: her usual temperament should return a little while after she has given birth. Whether this change in temperament occurs or not, you should avoid picking her up unless absolutely necessary, as it places pressure on her delicate abdomen.

FALSE PREGNANCIES

As mentioned earlier in this chapter, female rabbits are prone to false pregnancies, which can be very distressing for them. False pregnancies occur for a number of reasons: the rabbit may have genuinely been pregnant but the foetuses died in early pregnancy; there may have been an unsuccessful mating; even the presence of a keen male nearby can trigger the effects of pregnancy.

False pregnancies can last for up to three weeks, during which time the doe may exhibit any or all of the signs of pregnancy – with the exception of a swollen abdomen. These include nest building and milk production. The latter can be very painful if your rabbit is not used to it, and may even lead to mastitis, which, in severe cases, will need to be treated by a vet.

If you are unsure whether your rabbit is undergoing a false pregnancy, take her to the vet, who will be able to tell by feeling the abdomen, or listening for heartbeats, whether any babies are present.

The best way to avoid false pregnancies is by spaying (see page 156).

THE BIRTH

The birth usually takes place at night and lasts between ten and thirty minutes, but it's not unheard of for some of the kittens to be born several hours – or even days – later. Your rabbit might give off some warning signs that the birth is imminent – these include frantically rearranging their nesting box and a general sense of restlessness.

If you are there at the birth, it is important that you do not interfere. If the doe becomes in any way stressed during the process, it can lead to rejection of the babies – in extreme cases the doe has been known to eat her young.

Each kitten is born with a placenta, which is eaten by the mother. She will then lick the babies clean and, once this happens, they should immediately start suckling. If any fragments of placenta remain, you should remove them.

More often than not, the birth is very straightforward, but there are certain birthing complications that you should be aware of. If you notice any of the following, you should immediately call your vet:

- A large amount of bleeding.
- If your doe cannot stand or appears otherwise weak.
- If your doe appears to be trying to give birth but nothing happens after several hours.
- If only a couple of kittens have come out, but your rabbit continues trying to give birth for a number of hours.
- If a kitten gets stuck in the process of coming out.

Any of these complications may need urgent attention, and your vet will be able to advise.

It is possible that, even though you are sure your rabbit was pregnant, you don't see any babies. Strange as it may sound, there are reasons for this. One is cannibalism (see page 167); the other is the process – not uncommon in rabbits – of reabsorption. This occurs when one or more of the gestating kittens die in the uterus and are reabsorbed into the rabbit's body. There can be environmental reasons for this happening – such as a poor diet – but in fact it is believed to be a very normal process. Some experts think that as many as half the foetuses are routinely reabsorbed, and it is possible that all of them will be.

THE BABIES

Litters can vary in size, and there are a number of factors that determine how many kittens your doe is likely to give birth to, including genetics and the general health of the mother. The average litter size, however, is five. Does have eight teats, so problems can arise if she gives birth to more than this number of young. In the wild, rabbits will kill the weaker babies if there are too many for them to nurse. This can also happen with domesticated rabbits, although excess kittens can be fostered out to other nursing mothers with young of about the same age; the other option is to take away the weakest specimens and have them put down by the vet.

Babies rely entirely on their mother's milk for the first few weeks of their lives, and when feeding their young, does may get through as much as three times the amount of food they normally eat and will drink copious amounts of water to maintain the flow of milk.

Baby rabbits are born blind, deaf and bald, apart from a very light covering of down. As tempting as it may be, don't handle the babies before they start emerging from the nest unless absolutely necessary – if one of them gets stranded outside the nest it is likely to catch hypothermia, for example. Any strange smells introduced through handling will alienate the babies from their mother, which will lead to them being rejected. If you must handle them, the best way to avoid this happening is to rub your hands in the existing hay to mask your own scent.

The kittens should open their eyes any time after about ten days, and two to three weeks into their lives they should start to leave the nest and eat small morsels of solid food, although they will continue to drink their mother's milk for a good six weeks. Rabbits' milk is very rich in nutrients, and the babies have enough space in their stomach to hold a fair amount in reserve, so don't be surprised if the mother is not in the nesting box all the time. This does not mean that she is rejecting her young; in fact, it is normal behaviour, often seen in the wild – if the mother stays with her young all the time, she may alert predators to their existence.

If your doe has difficulty feeding her young, rejects them or dies in childbirth, it is possible to bottle-feed the babies, although you will need to consult your vet about this. They will recommend a special formula milk that contains all the nutrients the babies need, as well as giving you specialist advice on how to go about it.

Once the kittens start venturing out of the nesting box, it is safe to start handling them. One of the first things you will want to do is determine what sex they are. To do this you need to look at their genitals. On a male, gentle pressure around the opening will reveal the penis; on females, naturally, it won't! That's the theory, but, because the genitals are relatively undeveloped at this stage, in practice it's not that simple and mistakes are frequently made. You should therefore check again when they reach about four months old to make sure you've got it right – even experienced vets can sex a rabbit incorrectly when it is very young.

The Tarrant household has had a couple of cases of mistaken identity with its rabbits! As you already know, Warren had to be renamed Warrenetta, and when I took Patchy Pete to the vet to be castrated, I found out that in fact she needed to be spayed – and is now fondly known as Patchy Petra.

Once the babies are fully weaned, which happens between six and ten weeks, they are ready to leave and that's when your potential owners should start preparing for their new arrivals. In the meantime, it is best to keep them in pairs, although young males should be separated from the age of about three months to stop any aggressive behaviour. Young rabbits should not be given too much green food or carrots to eat, as it can damage their underdeveloped digestive system. Make sure that they are eating plenty of hay, and gradually introduce small quantities of green food.

WHAT CAN GO WRONG?

Does, especially those that have never had a litter before, are not necessarily natural mothers, so there are things that can go wrong. The first of these, which is always rather abhorrent to humans, is cannibalism. Simply speaking, the doe gives birth to her litter and immediately eats them. There are a number of possible reasons for this, including an inadequate diet or stress. The truth is, however, that cannibalism occurs in the wild for, it is thought, good reasons. If a mother believes that the arrival of youngsters is likely to attract predators to the colony, or if there is not enough food to go round, she may eat her young out of a sense of self-preservation. If your doe does this once, it may be that she is genetically predisposed to this behaviour, so you should not continue breeding her.

If the birth all goes according to plan, but you notice any of the following symptoms in one or more of the kittens, you should consult your vet, as it could be a sign of something serious:

- Unopened eyes after ten days
- Diarrhoea
- Runny nose
- Brown urine
- Crying
- No movement

CONTINUING THE BREEDING PROCESS

Once your doe has given birth, she may accept the amorous attentions of a buck only a couple of days afterwards. Whether or not she is capable of becoming pregnant again so soon largely depends on the size of her litter: if she has a very small litter, she will become pregnant fairly easily; if she has a larger litter, she may become pregnant, but nature will terminate the pregnancy after a few days.

However, just because a doe can become pregnant again so soon after giving birth, it should not be encouraged. Her health and longevity will undoubtedly suffer if she is forced to suckle her young and be pregnant at the same time, and this kind of intensive breeding, as I have said before, is incredibly irresponsible. Does really should not be allowed to become pregnant more than three times a year at the very maximum.

Lisa Maxwell

A Bunny for Beau

As DC Samantha Dixon in ITV's *The Bill*, Lisa Maxwell is pretty clued up on the law of the land; but when it comes to rabbits she confesses to knowing nothing. She didn't know that rabbits could live indoors or that they could be trained to understand basic commands, so was pleasantly surprised to discover that they are more than just big-

eared, big-eyed, big-toothed animals with little brains!

All I know about rabbits is that they live wild in the New Forest and that they bring enormous pleasure to my daughter Beau. I have never owned a rabbit, so other than that – and the fact that they eat carrots – I really don't know anything about them. When I was told that they bite, I remembered being bitten by a hamster once and not being able to get it off my finger, so I thought, Imagine what a rabbit can do with those great big teeth!

I am a townie and grew up on a council estate in the Elephant and Castle, in south-east London, so the chances of me seeing a rabbit that wasn't cooked were few and far between. I could never eat one though. The whole idea that rabbits are funny, cute little bunnies put me off – I wouldn't even eat Welsh rarebit because I grew up thinking it was rabbit on toast!

Because I was brought up with cats and dogs, I understand them, so they would ordinarily always be my first choice of pet. My partner Paul also grew up with dogs – West Highland Terriers – so we both erred in favour of a dog and chose a Miniature Schnauzer. But Beau wanted a rabbit. She has always wanted one. Her first introduction to rabbits was at school, where most children are introduced to small pets. Rabbits hold an incredible magic for little children. I can see how much pleasure they bring to Beau and her friends, but I think cats and dogs bring them more enjoyment, so kids don't see rabbits as pets – they just want to play with them like toys.

Beau is mad on animals and, because we can bring the school rabbit home for weekends or holidays, I am going to start with that. That will give us an idea of what is really involved in looking after a rabbit, and we will learn all about feeding, bedding, cleaning and grooming. I'm looking forward to it, and so is Beau.

If all goes well caring for the school rabbit, we'll then do our own careful research into what kind of breed and size of rabbit would be suitable for us, what other equipment we will need and which vaccinations the rabbit will require.

I have a great respect for animals, including rabbits, so I would never take on ownership of a pet lightly. They are a huge responsibility and we thought long and hard before deciding to get our dog. It's a similar thought process to starting a family, only at a much lower level. Having Beau completely changed our lives around but now, if I were to have another child, it wouldn't make such a huge difference. Now that we have one pet, getting a rabbit for Beau isn't a problem and, if she got bored with it, that won't be a problem either. My only worry is that that I won't be able to look after it properly myself. I know people keep them outside in hutches but I don't like the idea of them being locked up and would worry about other pets and animals getting at it. I don't even like cats and dogs being left outside but, because rabbits are clean and

THE RABBIT WHISPERER

Beau is besotted with them, I can't think of a better pet for her to have as her own. I just hope the one we choose won't bite our fingers off!

8

The Rabbit in the House

Traditionally, rabbits live in hutches – but they don't have to. In the past thirty years, more and more have become popular house pets, much like cats and dogs, and they can live alongside humans with the greatest of ease. This is fantastic news for both rabbits and owners – as long as you know what you are doing. Indeed, there are definite advantages to bringing your rabbit in from the cold!

The first advantage of having a house rabbit is that it is more fun, both for you and the rabbit. Rabbits are naturally sociable creatures, so living indoors will make them feel more like one of the family, and will ensure that you get more out of having a pet rabbit than you would otherwise. The second advantage is one of health. Indoor living is not necessarily better for rabbits than outdoor living per se, but it does have one obvious benefit: you will see it more and therefore be more likely to notice if there are any signs of illness. Finally, there is the ongoing issue of safety. Rabbits in the great outdoors are naturally prey to all manner of predators and, even though they may be safely cooped up in their hutches, they are sensitive souls: the very presence of a predator around them can literally scare them to death.

However, if you are going to keep a house rabbit, you need to be aware of a number of issues. First off, a house rabbit really should be neutered. You also need to make sure that the accommodation and environment provided will make the rabbit feel comfortable and secure. Once the rabbit is in the home, you will need to fully house-train it; and you must be certain that your house is fully bunny-proofed, both for the safety of the rabbit and for your own peace of mind. Let's look at each of these issues in turn.

NEUTERING

Both male and female house rabbits should be neutered. It is even more important than with outdoor rabbits. For a start, they will be easier to house-train. Also, castrating restricts the buck's tendency to spray urine in order to mark out their territory. It also makes them much less aggressive, so that they can live in harmony with your family and also any other household pets and rabbits you may have. For a more detailed discussion on the benefits of neutering, see page 156.

ACCOMMODATION

Indoor accommodation for rabbits is quite different to outdoor accommodation, although it does need to fulfil many of the same criteria. So, rather than needing a large hutch, a smaller box or appropriate cage will suffice, which can be put in a closed-off area of a room and act as a nesting box, enabling your rabbit to hide away when it feels the need to do so. You should also supply a litter tray – see the section on house-training on page 176.

The cage should be lined with newspaper, in the same way that you would line an outdoor hutch, and filled with hay or straw. For some, the mess created by these materials is unacceptable indoors, so you could substitute it with a synthetic pet fleece, which is soft, cosy, warm and washable. The rabbit will, however, still need hay to eat, so I would recommend buying a hay rack. This is a V-shaped rack that clips on to the side of the cage and holds the hay your rabbit needs for a healthy diet. It makes it easily accessible for the rabbit – yet more challenging as it may have to get up on its hind legs to get at the hay – and will prevent your pet from spreading it all around the house.

As with outdoor hutches, you should provide a water bottle (don't forget to change it every day!) and a food bowl that should be heavy enough to stop your rabbit tipping it over.

Positioning of the cage is something you should consider well. We have already discovered that rabbits can tolerate colder temperatures, but they do not respond well to excessive heat or to sudden changes in temperature. For this reason you should make sure the cage is out of the way of direct sunlight, which can quickly cause heatstroke, is not placed anywhere near a heat source such as a radiator and is well out of the way of any draughts. Make sure the cage is in a room where there is not generally a lot of noise or activity. While all your rabbits will enjoy being part of the household, and will like to watch the comings and goings of the family, they will still be guided by their natural timidity and will not appreciate being around boisterous children, loud music or constant television.

HOUSE-TRAINING YOUR RABBIT

Rabbits that are largely kept outdoors will perform their natural functions where they please but, indoors, you should train them to go where it pleases you, and where it is clean and hygienic. Fortunately, rabbits are creatures of habit and so are quite easy to house-train, particularly if they have been neutered.

For hygiene and convenience, it is best to get a litter tray. This should be large enough for the rabbit to sit in comfortably – you can buy a small cat litter tray from a pet shop, and fill it with sand, wood shavings, soil or special rabbit litter. Don't use cat litter however: it is quite dusty and has a tendancy to clump, which, if nibbled or eaten, could cause an internal blockage. Keep bunny restricted to its boundaries for the first few days, and move any droppings or wet areas into the litter tray. You will find that the rabbit will start to use the tray of its own volition. Once it does, you can let the rabbit out for a short period of time and gradually increase the time it is allowed out each day. There are bound to be a few small accidents, but generally rabbits get the hang of it quite quickly and will return to the tray each time 'nature' calls.

BUNNY-PROOFING YOUR HOUSE

Rabbits are nosy little things, and will want to start exploring every nook and cranny of your house and, while this is to be expected, you need to ensure that it is safe for it to do so – and safeguard your precious possessions at the same time. Rabbits will try to chew anything, so you need to second-guess what they are likely to go for, and either remove it or protect it. Providing a chewing block in the rabbit's cage will go some way to stopping indiscriminate nibbling, but it will not by any means eliminate it entirely.

Other favourite things to nibble include wooden furniture legs, skirting boards and loose rugs or carpets – anything, in fact, that the rabbit finds on its own level. For this reason it helps to limit their freedom to a couple of rooms that have been made totally safe. Pay particular attention to danger zones where your rabbit might become stuck and injure itself. The best way to do this is to get down on all fours and try to see the world through the eyes of a rabbit. You can bunny-proof certain everyday household objects as follows:

FURNITURE LEGS

Some people recommend protecting wooden furniture legs with sturdy plastic sheeting, clingfilm or bubble wrap, but I wouldn't advise this as plastic is indigestible and dangerous to rabbits and all other animals and could ultimately kill them. For this reason, fabric would be better but it is also unsightly, so I would recommend spraying furniture legs with a special anti-chewing repellent, available from pet shops. Personally, I don't use either fabric or repellent – my rabbit soon learned that, if I said 'no', or clapped my hands, it must stop.

CARPETS

Make sure there are no loose edges for your rabbit to get hold of – this means making sure all carpets are securely tacked down. Loose rugs are asking for trouble – if they are precious to you, do not have them in rooms where your rabbit is allowed. However, you could put down cheap rugs to divert your rabbit's attention from other more precious objects in the house.

WALLPAPER

Rabbits love to nibble at paper, so make sure there are no loose bits of wallpaper that your rabbit can easily bite off and tear.

ELECTRICAL WIRES

Rabbits also love wires, so these should be well out of reach of your rabbit, or covered with a protective sheath: it can be incredibly dangerous if it gnaws through a live wire. Not only does the rabbit run the risk of electrocuting itself, there is also a possibility that this will start a fire in your house.

HOUSE PLANTS

By nature, rabbits nibble plants, leaves and greens, so houseplants are an obvious target. It's best to remove them but, if you do want to keep your plants in a room where a rabbit is allowed to be, move them out of reach and, as an added precaution, check the list of poisonous plants on page 207 to make sure you are not putting the rabbit at risk.

HEAVY OBJECTS

This is something that many people forget: a heavy object on a precarious table can be a very great danger to a rabbit nosing around the table's feet. Make sure you don't leave anything around that puts your rabbit at risk of being clonked on the head, or, worse, squashed!

BURNS

Rabbits are natural scavengers, so they will be attracted to any hot food and drinks left around. Make sure you are not putting your rabbit at risk of being burned or scalded by leaving cups of hot tea etc. within their reach.

TRAINING YOUR RABBIT

It is perfectly possible to train your rabbits to obey certain commands in much the same way you might train a dog or a cat. Rabbits are quite intelligent little things and, being creatures of habit, they learn quickly. If you see your pet approaching a tasty-looking table leg, or a more dangerous-looking electrical cord, say 'no' to it in a gentle but firm voice. If it still makes a beeline for the object of its desire, pick the rabbit up and move it. It will soon learn what 'no' means! You could also try squirting it with a bit of water to discourage it, thereby distancing yourself a bit from being the disciplinarian.

You can also encourage your rabbit not to eat forbidden things by leaving a selection of chewable objects and toys around the rooms it is allowed into – that way, the rabbit is entertained and both of you are happy!

TAKING AN INDOOR RABBIT OUT

There is absolutely no reason why a house rabbit has to stay indoors all the time. In any case, it is not natural and a rabbit kept indoors will positively relish the opportunity to explore the smells and sounds of the outdoor world. You need to take the same precautions that you would with an outdoor rabbit. There should be no means of escape or any poisonous plants and, if you don't have a well-protected rabbit run, you should accompany it at all times to avoid any interference from its many natural predators. Remember that indoor rabbits are not conditioned to outdoor climates, so, to make the transition less extreme, you might take your house rabbit out in the summer rather than the winter. As it gets colder, they will naturally start acclimatising, so there is no reason why they can't be taken outdoors most of the year round.

BRINGING AN OUTDOOR RABBIT IN

It may be that you have an outdoor rabbit and would like to bring it inside and train it as a house rabbit. This is perfectly possible, but you do need to think this through.

To start with, you might want to consider bringing the rabbit's hutch inside for a while, rather than introducing it to an inside cage immediately. This will make the transition a bit easier for your pet. The next thing you need to think about is house-training. The instructions on page 176 still hold for this situation, but bear in mind that it may take a little longer if your rabbit is very stuck in its ways.

The most important consideration, however, is one of temperature. We know that rabbits can manage at fairly low temperatures, but they find hotter temperatures more difficult. If your rabbit has been used to living its life outdoors, it may find the sudden change in temperature difficult to get used to. If you can, make the transition during spring or autumn. Not only will the difference in temperature be smaller when it is getting cooler or warmer outside, but also your rabbit will be better able to cope with the indoor warmth because it will be either shedding or growing its winter coat. If you do make the transition in summer, however, you still need to be aware of your rabbit's needs. Try and choose the coolest room in the house. North-facing rooms are best because they are not in direct sunlight during the day. South-facing rooms and conservatories are a bad idea – they heat up like greenhouses, which is very unhealthy for rabbits.

Mike Batt

Bright Eyes

Is it a kind of a dream,
Floating out on the tide,
Following the river of death downstream?
Oh, is it a dream?

THE RABBIT WHISPERER

There's a fog along the horizon,
A strange glow in the sky,
And nobody seems to know where it goes,
And what does it mean?
Oh, is it a dream?

Bright eyes, burning like fire.
Bright eyes, how can you close and fail?
How can the light that burned so brightly
Suddenly burn so pale,
Bright eyes?

Is it a kind of a shadow,
Reaching into the night,
Wandering over the hills unseen,
Or is it a dream?

There's a high wind in the trees,
A cold sound in the air
And nobody ever knows when you go,
And where do you start
Oh, into the dark?

Bright eyes, burning like fire.
Bright eyes, how can you close and fail?
How can the light that burned so brightly
Suddenly burn so pale,
Bright eyes?

Bright eyes, burning like fire.
Bright eyes, how can you close and fail?
How can the light that burned so brightly
Suddenly burn so pale,
Bright eyes?

Recognise the words? This classic ballad, recorded by Art Garfunkel, was written and composed by Mike Batt as the soundtrack for *Watership Down*. The film, based on the book written by Richard Adams, is about a colony of rabbits that face an uncertain future when their warren, Sandleford, is about to be destroyed by property developers. Richard Adams grew up in Newbury near the Berkshire Downs, where *Watership Down* is set. In the book he weaves his knowledge of the area and facts about rabbits into the fictitious plot, which concentrates on a brave bunch of Berkshire bunnies that flee from Sandleford and go in search of a safe haven where they can create a new home. Written from the perspective of rabbits in the wild, it highlights how their lives are affected when man interferes with the environment.

Rabbits, like other animals, have a strong sixth sense so, when Fiver senses that something dreadful is about to happen, it is not without foundation. While the rest of the family of rabbits are left powerless to defend themselves against the bulldozers, Fiver, his brother Hazel and a group of friends set off on a perilous journey to Watership Down. These brave bunnies face the very real problems encountered by moving into unfamiliar territory and must deal with their natural enemies, including other rabbits, which are known to fiercely defend their territory against new arrivals.

By giving rabbits the power of speech, the analogy between rabbits in the wild and humans highlights how far-reaching the detrimental affects on our environment become.

So did composer, lyricist and singer Mike Batt need to get inside a rabbit's head to get the inspiration to write the words and music for 'Bright Eyes'?...

... No, and, even if I had remembered that my children Luke and Hayley had two rabbits, I would not have looked to them for any inspiration! Thinking of it now, I am not even sure if the rabbits are still alive!

All I was told was that *Watership Down* would be an animated film about rabbits used as a human analogy and my brief, quite simply, was to compose and write a song about death!

When Richard Adams wrote the book, he was thinking about rabbits that could be human but when I wrote 'Bright Eyes' I was only thinking of humans, so the imagery created by the words 'Following the river of death downstream' and 'There's a fog along the horizon' is nebulous. 'Bright Eyes' can be applied to any human or animal so it covers every perspective.

We chose Art Garfunkel as the singer because he was already established as an international star and known for his sensitive songs. It reached number one in ten countries around the world including the UK, where it remained for six weeks, which might have been hard to achieve if anyone else had recorded it.

After the film was released there was a story going round about a butcher who had a row of dead rabbits displayed in his shop window with a notice underneath that read: 'You've read the book. You've seen the film. Now eat the cast!'

'Bright Eyes' Words and Music by Mike Batt
©1978, reproduced by permission of EMI Songs Ltd, London WC2H 0QY

9

Rabbit Trivia

September 27 is International Rabbit Day.

Rabbits are the third most popular pet in the UK.

A colony of 407 rabbits was once found living in a warren with 2,080 exits.

Thumper, Flopsy and Charlie are the most popular rabbit names.

The highest a rabbit has jumped is an astonishing eighteen inches! This record is held by Golden Flame, a three-year-old Satin from West Sussex who set the new record high in August 2002.

Twenty-four rabbits were introduced to Australia in 1859. Now there are approximately 300 million!

Rabbits take up to eighteen naps a day.

Rabbits can reach a speed of 47mph.

Rabbits are incapable of vomiting.

A rabbit's eyes can see in every direction so it can see a bird in the sky as well as a predator on the ground at the same time.

In Chinese mythology rabbits are a symbol of longevity. In reality, the natural lifespan of a rabbit is no more than a few years but, as a species, they have been around for millions of years.

In different cultures, rabbits are associated variously with love, fertility, victory of wit over brawn, and cowardice.

The VW Golf was sold and marketed as the VW Rabbit in North America.

Welsh Rabbit is melted cheese on toast not, as the name suggests, an actual rabbit on toast! Rarebit is a euphemism for the faint-hearted

In Cockney rhyming slang 'rabbit' means 'talk' – rabbit and pork, talk!

A popular ragtime dance in the early 1900s was the bunny hop, so called because (with a little stretch of the imagination) it resembled the movements of a choreographed rabbit!

'Rabbit' is an historical British slang expression referring to an incompetent sports person – usually a cricketer or tennis player.

It is thought that the word 'bunny' comes from the seventeenth-century Gaelic word for a rabbit's tail: a bun.

In the 1960s Hugh Heffner created the infamous Bunny Girls, the casino/nightclub hostesses who were identified by their black satin bodices with white fluffy tails and traditional big bunny ears to complete the ensemble. Synonymous with naughty but nice, the silhouette of a bunny's head was recognised as an emblem of Heffner's global Playboy empire, which at its height had forty clubs worldwide and owned the popular top-shelf magazine *Playboy*.

There are various theories as to why rabbits are commonly associated with Easter. The word Easter is a derivative of Eastre (or Ostera), the Teutonic Goddess of Dawn and the Dawning of Spring who was believed to have opened the doors of Valhalla for the slain god Baldur in order to bring light to the world. When spring arrived after the long, dark winter months and life returned to earth, the ancient Saxons believed that it heralded Eastre's return which they celebrated by holding a feast in her honour – the festival of Eastre. Rabbits were sacred to Eastre so, when Christians adopted her name, they also adopted her traditional rabbit in keeping with the association. Another theory is that rabbits, by their sheer fecundity, are a symbol of fertility and, as spring is the most fertile season of the year, represent productive growth.

THE RABBIT WHISPERER

Children are traditionally told that, if they are good, the Easter bunny will bring them eggs on the eve of Easter for them to find on Easter morning, just like Father Christmas brings presents on Christmas Eve.

The luckiest amulet charm of all is considered to be the rabbit's foot. To be truly lucky, it must be the left hind foot of a rabbit that has been killed by a cross-eyed person at the time of the full moon, and it must be carried in the left pocket! As the hind legs are longer and stronger than the forelegs, they were considered to carry unusual powers and were carried to ward off harmful forces, ill health and witchcraft. Carrying one at all times was also thought to prevent gout!

Brushing a rabbit's foot on the face of a newborn child or keeping one in its pram is traditionally believed to ward off evil spirits, and keeping one under a baby's pillow is thought to prevent accidents.

The traditional cure for cramp is to rub the bone of a rabbit's foot in circular movements over the area!

A traditional cure for rheumatism is carrying the right forefoot of a rabbit in your pocket!

Samuel Pepys used a rabbit's foot to cure his recurrent stomach aches, but it is not known whether he ate the foot or rubbed it across his belly!

On the opening night of a play, superstitious actors will apply their make-up with a rabbit's foot then kiss it and rub it over their face and hands for luck. An actor must never lose a rabbit's foot. If he does, he loses his talent.

African slaves regarded rabbits as mystical and believed that rubbing the left foot of a rabbit brought good luck.

Some people believe that seeing a rabbit is bad luck, and that the antidote is to spit over your shoulder.

In Welsh folklore, seeing a white hare, rabbit, weasel or mole was a forewarning of misfortune.

In regions of Northwest America and British Columbia, seeing a rabbit signified a period of peace.

If a rabbit crosses your path from right to left, the journey will be disastrous. If it crosses from left to right it is a lucky sign. If it runs along the road in front of you, what you set out to achieve that day may not happen and remain unaccomplished for some time.

Folklore dictates that, if a farmer or his wife sees a rabbit on a May morning, their cows won't produce milk that day.

If a rabbit's fur is thick in autumn, farmers take it as a sign of a hard winter ahead. A thin coat suggests it will be mild.

Inhabitants on the Isle of Portland in Dorset, England, believe that rabbits bring the worst form of bad luck, and so accept that, if a quarryman sees a rabbit on his way to work, he will immediately return home and take the day off. So superstitious are these Portlanders that they will never say the word 'rabbit'. Instead, they refer to them as 'one of them furry things' or 'Wilfred'. Their biggest insult is to say 'Rabbits to you.'

Should a rabbit or hare cross in front of a bride, it is a bad omen.

Wicked witches were thought to be able to turn people into animals and transform themselves into a black cat or a rabbit. It was therefore considered very bad luck if anyone saw a black rabbit. Rabbits seen on any May morning are thought to be witches. If a rabbit was hard to skin, they were thought to have been exceptionally evil witches. Therefore in Welsh folklore they would say, 'This old witch had many sins to answer for.'

A rabbit seen running down a street or through a village was a forewarning that a house in the immediate vicinity would catch light. Others reckoned it was bad luck to have a rabbit run through your garden because your house would catch fire before the end of the year.

The superstition that rabbits are unlucky at sea dates back to the seventeenth century when, according to legend, hundreds of people drowned when a warship sank after one of the rabbits which had been brought aboard for food gnawed a hole through the hold. Consequently, some fishermen believe that disaster is sure to follow if a rabbit or any part of rabbit's body is on board their boats. If a fisherman found a rabbit in his net he would burn it rather than go to sea with it. Even going to sea with any part or bit of fur from a rabbit is very unlucky – a story dating back to 1930 tells how boys effectively prevented their fathers from going to sea by getting hold of rabbit skins, filling them with rubbish and placing them in the sterns of boats! For sailors, a dead rabbit on board a ship or boat would bring bad weather. If someone so much as said the word 'rabbit' while at sea, they would return to harbour as fast as possible in case something dreadful happened. Instead, they referred to them as 'those hairy things'. To avoid having to say the word 'rabbit' on board, when talking about Rabbit Island sailors referred to it as Gentleman's Island.

When meat rationing was introduced to England in World War Two, the then Minister of Food, Lord Woolton allowed people to raise chickens and rabbits in their back gardens – essentially to supplement the mainly vegan diet with protein. However, this led to neighbourly competitions being held to see who could produce the finest specimens so, in this respect, it could be said that Lord Woolton was inadvertently responsible for promoting the considerable growth of hobbyists and fancy rabbit (and chicken) breeders that exist in the UK today! Naturally, chicken and rabbit were the main dishes of the day and none so tasty as Ye Olde English Rabbit Stew served with home grown potatoes!

For a lucky month ahead, you should say 'Rabbits' three times just before going to sleep on the last day of the month, then 'Hares' three times as soon as you wake up next morning. If you say 'black cats' on the last night of the month and 'white rabbits' next morning, you will get a present before the end of that month.

The first trick that inspired the ongoing use of rabbits in magic was performed in 1796 by Mary Toft of Godalming, Surrey who allegedly gave birth to nine baby rabbits.

Had it not been witnessed by her local doctor, John Howard, it would have been written off as the wild imaginings of an insane woman and never gone any further. Instead, he wrote to several eminent doctors in England telling them that he had seen his patient giving birth to parts of nine dead baby rabbits and, trusting they would respect the word of a fellow doctor, asked them to investigate this medical mystery. On hearing this, King George I sent his own anatomist, Nathanael St. Andre and Samuel Molyneux, secretary to the Prince of Wales. During their investigations she continued giving birth to parts of rabbits, confirming Dr Howard's bizarre story. Mary further informed them that while she was pregnant she had developed a craving for rabbit meat, but because it was so hard to get, she started having dreams that they were sitting on her lap.

To further their investigations, doctors put one of the lungs from the still-born rabbits into water to see if it would float. Amazingly they ignored the significance that it did: this meant that it must have breathed in air and therefore at some point have been alive outside the womb. Bewildered, they sent her to London to be seen by London's top physician, Sir Richard Manning, where she was kept under constant observation but stopped producing. By now her medical case had become a national sensation. Crowds surrounded the house where she was being kept, but stories that people in Mary's village had supplied her husband with rabbits were beginning to surface.

While waiting for Sir Richard Manning to carry out tests on her uterus, she confessed to the truth and told them that, while no one was looking, she had inserted the dead rabbits inside her womb. What she really craved was fame and to get a pension from the King! She certainly achieved fame, but instead of a pension she was found guilty of fraud and sent to prison. Mary Toft tricked the nation and inspired magicians to continue using rabbits in their tricks. Fortunately for her, she was released without trial shortly afterwards and, a year later, gave birth to a healthy human.

When Simon Steggal fell into a diabetic coma, his wife Victoria thought he was snoozing in front of the TV and went into the kitchen but their giant 3-foot 21lb house rabbit Dory sensed there was something wrong and saved his life by raising the alarm.

Dory, who had been with the Steggal family for four months, had just been chastised by Victoria for scratching the furniture, so when she heard him doing it again she went back into the sitting room to investigate and found Dory sitting on Simon's lap scratching at his shirt, licking his face and thumping on his chest. Realising something was wrong, she phoned for paramedics who gave him an emergency injection which brought him back to consciousness – thanks to Dory.

Rabbits' teeth grow and grow so it is important for them to chew on hay and grass, logs and hard pellets to grind them down and keep them trimmed.

Just like you, rabbits need friends – furry, human or both! In the wild they live in colonies and are therefore naturally sociable creatures.

Beatrix Potter kept her pet rabbits Peter Piper and Benjamin Bouncer indoors.

Grass contains everything a rabbit needs to keep it healthy. Rabbits scatter their droppings over the grass not only to warn other rabbits that this is their territory but also to fertilise the grass they eat.

When a rabbit is aware of danger, he 'thumps' his back leg to warn other rabbits

Rabbits should be called 'habits'! They will always go to the toilet in the same areas, which is why they are so easy to house-train.

When a rabbit is happy it will make a purring sound using its teeth.

Rabbits don't like being picked up, especially from above. Being prey animals they are naturally nervous of anything that swoops down on them. When you pick up your rabbit always approach it at ground level and from the side where it can see you.

Like other prey animals, a rabbit's eyes are situated on each side of the head and designed to function independently of each other. They can therefore see separate things from different angles, both laterally and behind, but, because they do not have stereoscopic vision like us, they cannot see anything directly ahead. To compensate for this blind spot, they detect food by using their lips and vibrissae, the sensitive stiff coarse hairs found beneath the mouth of most mammals.

Scent is much more important to rabbits than sight and sound. Each has its own scent profile and all are capable of distinguishing between familiar and unfamiliar humans as well as their gender!

A rabbit has 17,000 taste buds whereas humans only have 10,000.

Rabbits' tails warn other rabbits of danger – as they run, the tail shows the white underneath which is used as a warning sign to other rabbits.

Rabbits are not rodents; they are lagomorphs.

THE RABBIT WHISPERER

There are over sixty recognised breeds of rabbit in the UK, but over 500 cross-breeds. There are more breeds of rabbit than any other domestic pet, with the exception of dogs.

A rabbit warren can have between 1 and 150 entrances.

Rabbits are fertile all year round.

In the nineteenth century, a 'rabbit skin' was a hood worn by an academic. A 'rabbit sucker' was a pawnbroker, and a 'rabbit-pie shifter' was a policeman.

The nineties expression 'bunny boiler' refers to any insanely jealous, predatory woman. It comes from the film *Fatal Attraction*, starring Glenn Close whose character becomes psychotically twisted when her lover, actor Michael Douglas, tries to end their passionate affair, she takes revenge by boiling his family's pet bunny.

CHINESE HOROSCOPES

Unlike the Western calendar, which has one of the twelve zodiac signs representing each month of the year, each year in the Chinese Calendar is represented by one of the twelve animal signs.

THE ORIGINS OF THE TWELVE ANIMALS

According to legend, Buddha had planned to hold the biggest party on earth since the animals disembarked from Noah's Ark and invited all the animals in the world to come. Unfortunately, only the Rat, Ox, Tiger, Rabbit (Hare), Dragon, Snake, Horse, Ram, Monkey, Rooster, Dog and Boar (Pig) made it, so, in honour of his twelve guests, Buddha rewarded them by naming a year after each one. The rabbit is the fourth animal sign and one of the luckiest animals in the chart.

People born in the Year of the Rabbit (which corresponds to Pisces in our Astrological chart) are peace-loving, sensitive and timid. They are good negotiators because they hate to fight and avoid dangerous situations wherever possible but if push comes to shove they will put up a courageous fight. They are said to be softly spoken, graceful and nimble, qualities that make them good politicians. True to nature, their best month is March and their best season is spring.

I was born in the year of the horse. We are cheerful, freedom-loving, independent, perceptive, fast-thinking and action-loving but we are bad time-keepers who jump before thinking and multi-task to the point of exhaustion.

THE RABBIT WHISPERER

Some of the famous people born in the Year of the Rabbit are:

Emperor Shi Huangdi, who built the Great Wall of China

Orson Welles, US actor, film and theatre director

Marie Antoinette, Queen of France (wife of Louis XVI) who died at the guillotine

Agatha Christie, the English murder mystery writer

King Olav V of Norway

Queen Victoria of England

Albert Einstein, founder of the theory of relativity

Andy Warhol, US artist, originator of Pop Art and film maker

Fidel Castro, Cuban revolutionary leader

Joseph Stalin, Russian dictator and founder of the Communist movement worldwide

Neil Sedaka, US singer and songwriter

David Rockefeller, descendant of the oil-rich family, once the richest in the world

Francis Ford Coppola, US film director

David Frost, political TV presenter

Dr Germaine Greer, feminist and author

Nanette Newman, English actress and writer (wife of film director, Brian Forbes)

Those born in 1903, 1915, 1927, 1939, 1951, 1963, 1975, 1987 and 1999 are all Rabbits. The next Year of the Rabbit will be in 2011.

The Year of the Rabbit signifies peace, prosperity and good luck.

The Rabbit Man

The Rabbit Man

How ironic that, when this man was sent to prison, he immediately plotted to release the Governor's rabbits from their rather impoverished existence and managed to secure a better quality of life for them behind bars.

THE RABBIT WHISPERER

You have to have been at Ford Open Prison for a certain length of time before you can ask for a particular job but when you are a new inmate, like I was, you have to go in front of a selection committee and be interviewed before they decide which job to give you. At the ripe old age of sixty, I couldn't see very well so I couldn't go into shirt-making because of my bad eyesight and I couldn't work in the fields or the vegetable patch because of my bad back. They offered me other posts but for various reasons, I couldn't do them either so they had to create a job for me and asked if I liked rabbits! 'To eat or look after?' I wanted to know. When they told me they could give me the job of looking after the Governor's rabbits, I leaped at the chance – if you know what I mean!

When I first took on the job, I was surprised to see that the rabbits had been rather neglected, so I set about making some changes and went to the department with a list of requests.

I asked them to get the best rabbit hutch money could buy for these little creatures, a decent run and proper containers for food and water – and got everything I asked for! I was thrilled.

With the job, I was given a bicycle and a special pass to go out and collect dandelion leaves in the adjoining fields. It gave me the freedom and licence to go anywhere and it also gave me the chance to pick us some mushrooms which I sneaked into my bucket!

I had about six rabbits and eight guinea pigs to look after which were kept in a run ostensibly to amuse the prisoners' children when they came on visiting days. It was a kind of kids' corner and they loved seeing the pets but quite a few came from rather rough families and threw stones at them which I immediately put a stop to, but was very careful when I chastised them in case they beat me up!

After the required length of time, I applied for and got a job in education but I wanted to continue looking after the pets. One of the prisoners was a heavyweight boxer and, when he heard I was looking for a helper, he asked if he could be my assistant. He loved it and, although you would never want to get on the wrong side of him, he had a heart of gold and became particularly fond of one of the rabbits. It was a lop-eared called Chelsea but one morning when we were all lining up for parade he suddenly leaped over the 15-foot prison wall to tell me he had gone to feed them and found her dead. Luckily, she was only asleep – but he was so upset, he was crying.

Everyone knew me as the Rabbit Man, which was appropriate because I soon got to know their mating habits and was always reading books to learn more about keeping and breeding them. I knew which plants and weeds were poisonous and which were safe. I loved it and, even to this day, I can spot a dandelion from 100 yards.

Appendix
Good and Bad Things to Eat

POISONOUS PLANTS

Rabbits can't just eat anything because it's green. There are a certain number of poisonous plants that you should make very sure your pet is not given or allowed near. These include:

Agave

Amaryllis

Anemone

Antirrhinum

Arum Lilies (aka Lords and
    Ladies

Autumn Crocus

Azalea

Bindweed

Bittersweet

Bluebells

Bracken

Bryony

Buttercup (unless dried and in
    small quantities)

Boxwood

Caladium

Celandine

Charlock

Chrysanthemum

Clematis

Columbine

Crocus

Cyclamen

Daffodil

Dahlia

Daphne

Delphinium

Dog Mercury

Figwort

Flowering dock leaves

Fool's Parsley

Foxgloves

Ground Elder

Hellebore

Hemlock

Henbane

Holly

Horsetails

Hyacinth

Iris

Ivy

Jerusalem Cherry

Juniper

Kingcup

Laburnum

Laurel

Leyland Cypress

Lily of the Valley

Lobelia

Lupin

Meadow Saffron

Monkshood

Morning Glory

Naked Lady

Narcissus

Nightshades (all types)

Oak leaves

Oleander

Poppy

Primrose

Poison Ivy

Privet

Ragwort

Rhododendron

Scarlet Pimpernel

Speedwell

Spurge

St John's Wort

Toadflax (also called Old
     Man's Beard)

Traveller's Joy (Wild
     Clematis)

Tulip

Wild celery

Wisteria

Wood Sorrel

Yew

GOURMET TREATS

There is nevertheless a huge range of both cultivated and wild plants that your rabbit will absolutely love, and some of these are listed below. Make sure you have read the section on feeding your rabbit (page 56) before you let it gorge!

Agrimony

Avens

Beetroot

Bramble

Broccoli

Brussels sprouts

Cabbage

Carrots

Cauliflower

Celery

Chickweed

Clover

Coltsfoot

Cow Parsnip

Dandelions

Fruit – all fruits can be given as treats

Goosegrass

Grass

Groundsel Knapweed

Lettuce (in very small quantities, as it is soporific)

Mallow

Mayweed

Plantain

Raspberry

Sea Beet

Shepherd's Purse

Sow Thistle

Spinach

Swede

Trefoil

Vetch

Watercress

Wild strawberry

Yarrow

Useful Contacts

THE RABBIT WELFARE
ASSOCIATION
PO Box 603
Horsham
West Sussex RH13 5WL
RWA Helpline: 0870 046 5249
www.rabbitwelfare.co.uk

The RWA is the fastest
growing, non-profit-making
rabbit organisation in the UK.
It offers both non-members
and over 7,000 members free
support, advice and tips on all
aspects of owning a rabbit. To
apply for membership, write to
the above address or phone.
Each year members will
receive four colourful issues of
'Rabbiting On' containing
features, articles and advice
from experts and other rabbit
owners, a RWA Members
Handbook, news on
conferences and shows
throughout the country and
access to their directory of
rescue shelters, rabbit-friendly
vets and boarding houses.

THE BRITISH RABBIT COUNCIL

Purefoy House
7 Kirkgate
Newark
Nottinghamshire NG24 1AD
Telephone: 01636 676042

Members of the BRC will receive fortnightly issues of 'Fur and Feather', (www.furandfeather.co.uk), designed for anyone interested in exhibiting rabbits as a hobby or owning as pets. It contains comprehensive reports on BRC-supported rabbit shows, help and advice on owning and breeding rabbits and a breeders' directory.

BLUE CROSS

Telephone: 01993 822651
www.bluecross.org.uk

This charitable organisation finds homes for pets and has animal hospitals in London and Grimsby. Under exceptional circumstances, free veterinary care is available to those living in these areas.

RSPCA

Wilberforce Way
Southwater
Horsham
West Sussex RH13 9RS
Telephone: 0870 3335 999
Fax: 0870 7530 284
RSPCA Cruelty Line:
0870 5555 999

The Royal Society of Prevention of Cruelty to Animals is a registered charity rescuing animals from harm and those at risk within the UK. They do not provide veterinary advice or treatment. Specific requests for leaflets should be made in writing, accompanied by two first class stamps to cover postage.
The enquiries service is open Monday to Friday, 9am to 5pm.

COTTON TAILS

Sherbourne House
Westbury
Wilstshire BA13 3JW
Telephone: 01370 864 222

Looking for a homeless bunny? Cotton Tails is an established non-profit-making sanctuary, housing approximately 30 rabbits. All are neutered and vaccinated before being rehomed. All staff work on a voluntary basis but a £25 donation is required to help meet veterinary costs, food and bedding.

PET PLAN LIFETIME RABBIT INSURANCE

Freepost SEA 5135
Computer House
Great West Road
Brentford TW8 9ZY
For advice and immediate cover telephone:
0800 072 7000 (calls are free)

A renewable annual subscription will ensure that the costs of each illness and injury are covered during each rabbit's lifetime.

THE HOUSE RABBIT SOCIETY (USA)

Founded in 1988, the HRS is an all-volunteer, national, non-profit animal rescue organisation based in Alameda, California, with local chapters in more than 30 states and more than 7,000 members. They foster, rescue and rehome abandoned rabbits and educate people into caring and understanding them as pets to reduce the number of unwanted rabbits.

Picture Credits

Colour plate section pictures all © Jane Burton/
Warren Photographic

Page 9 picture of Alice Beer © Amanda Searle

Page 41 picture of Toyah Willcox © Sven Arnstein/Stay Still

Page 65 picture of Nick Ferrari © Nic Gaunt, reproduced by
kind permission of LBC 97.3

Page 87 picture of Chris and Ingrid Tarrant © Ingrid Tarrant

Page 105 picture of Paul O'Grady © Nicky Johnston, ITV

Page 123 picture of Paul Daniels © Ian Spratt

Page 149 picture of Andrew Castle © Alan Olley/
Scopefeatures.com

Page 169 picture of Lisa Maxwell and Beau: Lisa Maxwell's
own collection

Page 183 picture of Mike Batt reproduced by kind permission
of Dramatico